How to survive the 9 to 5

Martin Lucas was a pig-farmer and university lecturer before he became a producer with Thames Television in 1978. He is particularly interested in producing TV programmes and books that help people to cope with real life more effectively. His previous books are *The Human Race* (with Terence Dixon) and *All in the Mind* (with John Nicholson).

Kim Wilson graduated in Mathematics and Philosophy from Churchill College, Cambridge. After working as an evening paper reporter, he joined BBC Wales as a radio producer. Progressing inexorably towards higher stress occupations he moved to Thames TV in 1984.

Emma Hart was educated at St Paul's Girls' School and Oxford University. She worked as a researcher at the Consumers' Association from 1977 to 1982, since when she has been at Thames TV.

Martin Lucas, Kim Wilson and Emma Hart

How to survive the 9 to 5

Thames Methuen

First published in Great Britain 1986
by Methuen London Ltd
11 New Fetter Lane, London EC4P 4EE
in association with
Thames Television International Ltd
149 Tottenham Court Road, London W1P 9LL
Copyright © 1986 Thames TV, Martin Lucas, Kim Wilson,
Emma Hart

Printed in Great Britain
by Richard Clay (The Chaucer Press) Ltd,
Bungay, Suffolk

British Library Cataloguing in Publication Data

Lucas, Martin
  How to survive the 9 to 5.
  1. Job stress
  I. Title II. Wilson, Kim III. Hart, Emma
  158.7   HF5548.85

  ISBN 0–423–01930–9

For Hilda, Charles and Marsha

Contents

Acknowledgements   ix

Introduction   1

1 What is stress?   5

2 Job satisfaction   25

3 Personality and stress   37

4 Personality and your job   52

5 Filers, foremen and fitters   72

6 Relationships   87

7 Keep smiling – the caring professions   101

8 The stress of change   113

9 The working woman   129

10 How to beat stress at work   143

Postscript   164

List of useful organisations   166

Select bibliography   170

Index   171

Acknowledgements

There are many people we and Professor Cooper would like to thank for their help in the making of this book and the TV series, but we'd particularly like to thank Carol Haslam and Channel Four for commissioning the series, and Clive Wood, John Nicholson and Tom Cox for all their ideas and encouragement. We'd also like to thank Peter Warr, Chris Clegg, Simon Norton, Malcolm Carruthers, Peggy Kellam, Sandra Kline, Mike Smith, Ivan Robertson and Ilan Baruch for so kindly helping us with research; Diana Potter and Ian Martin for all their interest and encouragement in the preparation of the TV series; and Nic Jones, Alex Bennion and Ann Mansbridge for their quite incredible achievement in converting this book from manuscript to paperback in a matter of weeks. We must also gratefully mention Cathy Olliver, Heather Wise and Sarah Collier, who put so much last-minute energy and effort into helping us convert our ideas into manuscript. Finally, of course, we are most grateful of all to the many working people quoted in this book who so freely and unself-consciously describe their feelings and experiences.

MARTIN LUCAS
KIM WILSON
EMMA HART

London 1985

Introduction

Studs Terkel in his acclaimed book *Working* describes what he sees to be the nature of work today:

> Work is, by its very nature, about violence – to the spirit as well as to the body. It is about ulcers as well as accidents, about shouting matches as well as fist fights, about nervous breakdowns as well as kicking the dog around. It is, above all (or beneath all), about daily humiliations. To survive the day is triumph enough for the walking wounded among the great many of us.

The sad thing about this quote is that for many jobs it is true. Work *is* dehumanising and unfulfilling. Only a small number of us are job-satisfied, while many of us suffer minor or major indignities in the workplace. This is partly to do with the way in which we are managed at work. We all seem to be managed more like machines than people. It may be that the technological age itself is creating men in the same images as machines. As Studs Terkel suggests later in his book, 'Perhaps it is this spectre that most haunts working men and women: the planned obsolescence of people that is of a piece with the planned obsolescence of the things they make. Or sell. It is perhaps this fear of no longer being needed in the world of needless things that most clearly spells out the unnaturalness, the surreality of much that is called work today.'

It may be glib to say that people are the most important resource that organisations possess. This is not only a humanistic reality, but a financial one as well. They make up a resource which should command a great deal of attention by top management, but frequently does not. Charles Handy in his book *Understanding Organisations* reflected on the implications of treating human beings as another form of capital asset:

Salaries and benefits are really regarded as maintenance expenses – something to be kept as low as possible as long as the machine does not break down. There is no capital cost and therefore no need for depreciation. Indeed, the return on investment of most companies would look very strange if their human assets were capitalised at, say, ten times their annual maintenance costs and depreciated over twenty years. Perhaps one day, industrial and administrative organisations will start behaving like football clubs and charge realistic transfer fees for their key people assets.

If people in the workplace are not properly managed, not only will their job satisfaction and motivation levels be low, but they are likely to suffer from stress-related illness as well. The cost to industry of stress-related disease is staggering. In the United States it is estimated at nearly $30 billion dollars a year just for stress-induced cardiovascular disease. In the United Kingdom, it has been calculated that industry loses millions of working days a year due to short-term stress-related illness, at a cost of many millions in national insurance and social security payments.

Regardless of the moral or humanistic or legalistic arguments, protecting the human asset should be a major concern of any enterprise from a cost-benefit point of view. In the United States, General Motors spend something like $2000 a year per employee on health care insurance, and over $1.3 billion overall (in 1978), which was a thirty-fold increase over 1960.

This book is meant to highlight the sources of job stress and what can be done about them. We will see that there are a number of potential sources of work-related stress, which extend from the way in which we are managed to our relationships at work generally. It is extremely important in any job, whether in the boardroom of a company or on the shop floor of a car assembly plant, to feel that you have some *control* over the everyday elements of your job. We attempt to explore the meaning and importance of control and participation in the workplace. Every effort is made to highlight work environments which are soul-destroying, as well as those that provide for individual growth and development. We also attempt to explore the importance of *relationships* at work. Relationships with our bosses, colleagues, subordinates and clients are extremely important if we are to be job-satisfied and to experience both physical and mental well-being at work.

There are a number of things that can be done to provide people with the kind of environment at work that helps them to develop as individuals, and to meet their own needs. Because of the enormous and escalating costs of job dissatisfaction, poor productivity and stress-related disease in industry, more and more companies must begin to provide career development guidance, participative decision-making in their companies, and stress prevention and counselling programmes. Many company doctors and personnel executives, who see the problems of stress at work, have found it difficult to implement stress management courses, counselling programmes etc – because senior executives feel that 'stress is none of our business' or 'he should be able to cope on his own' or 'our responsibility is to make profits for our shareholders, not to mollycoddle our employees'.

If British industry is not only to survive the 1980s and 1990s, but to remain competitive and keep its employees well motivated, it must change. Change is the name of the game. Change means thinking about the most important resource organisations have – its *people*. All organisations, whether in the public or private sector, must look at the human resource differently in the future. They must not only select the right people for the right job, but motivate and support them as well. If we truly care about the human resource, then we must demonstrate this concern with action. We must keep in mind Studs Terkel's words when he described work as being 'about a search, too, for daily meaning as well as daily bread, for recognition as well as cash, for astonishment rather than torpor; in short, for a sort of life rather than a Monday through Friday sort of dying'.

Professor Cary L. Cooper
December 1985

CHAPTER ONE

What is stress?

In the last few years nearly everyone has heard something about stress, especially stress at work and the fact that it can make you physically or mentally ill or even kill you. You've probably also heard that a certain amount of stress is good for everyone, that there is such a thing as 'positive stress', and that some people thrive on any stress or even go so far as to seek it out. But what is stress, anyway? How is it really different from the ordinary feelings of tension and pressure that everyone experiences at least some of the time at work and in their life generally? How can you tell if what you or your colleague at work are experiencing really is damaging stress, or whether you're just worrying too much about worry?

What stress isn't

We can list first some of the things that stress certainly *isn't*. For example, feeling that you are having *demands* made on you isn't necessarily a source of stress. Many workers welcome challenges made to their abilities and, providing they eventually feel that they can rise to meet those challenges, they will gain in confidence, 'muscle' and skill.

Being *anxious* about your capacity to cope with the demands on you is not the same thing as being under stress. Any sensible person will occasionally find themselves in situations where they will, quite rightly, feel that if they don't act quickly things could go wrong. Being anxious can be a valuable warning signal that it's time to re-evaluate a situation, and the ability to do this may well be a means of ultimately preventing stress.

A large work *load* is not necessarily a source of stress either – many people thrive on vast amounts of work and working long hours. Being extremely involved in the job you are doing is not the same thing as being stressed. And being in a work situation where you can't tell what's going to happen next and where the outcome could be a major reverse or gain in your fortunes is not necessarily a stressful situation – if this were the case people wouldn't spend so much time gambling.

Even having responsibility for large amounts of money, or people's health or even their lives, is not necessarily a source of stress. Many money-dealers, bank managers, doctors or nurses couldn't bear to do a less responsible job. We know also that having an anxious, worrying sort of personality is not the same thing as being a stress-vulnerable person. Many of the people doing some of the most demanding jobs around have been anxious since the day they were born, but they are not necessarily stressed. And being in conflict with everyone else around you doesn't necessarily cause stress. Many executives and managers cope with constant negotiations and arguments – in fact they may even prefer them and arrange their work lives so they can have lots of competitive meetings.

Finally, being bored and fed up with your job is not necessarily the same thing as finding it stressful. Many shop-floor workers in Britain are compelled to do nasty, boring, repetitive work – but not all of them are stressed.

What stress is

Quite apart from how you may consciously feel about your job and yourself, the most useful way to understand stress and what's most important about it, is that it's something that makes you physically or mentally *ill*. It's very difficult to make sweeping generalisations about what will make a particular person ill, but one or two very basic points seem to be clear.

All living creatures interact in some way with the world around them. One of their main tasks is to get what they want out of the environment and make sure that all the ups and downs and changes that happen around them don't constantly upset them. You could say that the reason why human beings are the most highly evolved of all animals is simply because, by using their brains and skills, they are so clever at both realising their aims and coping with the complicated changes and demands that occur all around them. In parallel with our brains, however, we have a much older homeostatic self-stabilising system of checks and balances in our bodies which does all sorts of useful things, like keep us warm when it's cold (or vice versa), give us extra energy when we want to act quickly, and so on. This same nervous and hormonal system puts us into overdrive when our brains tell us that we are going to have to cope with excessive demand. It's a kind of reserve capacity.

This system (known by scientists as the sympathetic nervous system) seems to have evolved to the point where it can wake us up, point out that there's a problem and nudge us into doing something dramatic about it – and it often works perfectly well. Indeed, feeling anxious and edgy about an unusual event, like the threat of a forthcoming redundancy, has been shown in at least one study of threatened workers, over a period of two and a half years, actually to *reduce* their chances of illness and unemployment. After the feared redundancy actually took place, by comparison the workers who *didn't* show this aroused response suffered more upsets and illnesses than the others.

However, people seem to become ill in various ways when this reserve capacity to adapt is consistently exploited over a long period, rather as a car, which can be driven at extra speed by leaving the choke out all the time, may eventually begin to show engine trouble. In human beings and other highly evolved animals this extended adaptation to a demand has been shown to proceed in three very well established phases. It begins with a period of *alarm*, followed by an extended period during which the organism rises to meet the extra demand; this is known as *resistance*. Finally, and sometimes without warning, there is a *collapse* into illness or exhaustion. However, the expression 'alarm' doesn't necessarily mean that people are consciously alarmed. This alarm manifests itself in changes in the balances between the brain, glands and organs – particularly as these balances are revealed by the hormones present in the blood. We now recognise a number of physical and mental symptoms which can also be observed in people who are beginning to go into the resistance stage of the stress cycle, even when they're not aware of it.

You might like to have a look at this checklist and see whether you are now suffering or have ever suffered from physical stress symptoms. Many people experience these symptoms but just don't recognise them as stress symptoms at all. Which of them apply to you?

Physical symptoms of stress

* I get spells of breathlessness, dizziness or nausea.
* I feel weepy and emotional or irritable.
* My appetite isn't what it used to be.
* I frequently suffer from indigestion.
* I suffer from constipation/diarrhoea.
* I have trouble getting to sleep, and often wake up early.
* I'm always tired.
* I sweat often and easily.
* I fidget and bite my nails.
* I get a lot of headaches or persistent pains in my back and neck.

If you recognise more than three of these symptoms in yourself you may have a stress problem – action might well be necessary. If you suffer from more than eight of the symptoms, you should think very seriously about taking immediate action. Visit your doctor, take time off work. Your health may be at risk.

How stress affects our bodies

When we perceive a situation as stressful a small pea-shaped body in the brain, called the hypothalamus, automatically signals the adrenal glands which are next to the kidneys to release the hormone adrenalin. This has various effects: it stimulates the heart and breathing rates, redirects the blood to the brain, heart and muscles, and, by narrowing the capillaries of the skin and stomach, it raises blood pressure.

A long list of internal activities all designed to optimise special effort go into operation. The liver dumps glucose into the blood by breaking down glycogen stores. The blood sugar level can reach a point under stress where sugar overflows into the urine causing temporary diabetes. Fatty acids – especially the kind called low-density lypo-protein cholesterol, which tends to accumulate in the linings of the blood vessels – are released from the liver, skin and gut. The stomach produces more acid and the spleen pushes more oxygen carrying red blood cells into the bloodstream. There's also an increase in fibrinogen and blood platelets which are designed to stop bleeding, and an increased production of the white blood cells which help repair body tissues.

How stress can make you feel good

Like almost every other system in our bodies, a check and balance mechanism called the parasympathetic nervous system operates in relation to arousal. When we perceive that an immediately worrying or demanding situation has gone away, our adrenals are increasingly stimulated to produce *nor*adrenalin, which acts as a brake on all the previously accelerated physiological processes, producing feelings of elation and relaxation.

Adrenalin might be called the 'get frightened and run away' hormone and noradrenalin the 'everything's OK, thank goodness' hormone. Many people actually get addicted to the feelings that noradrenalin produces in them, and certain jobs by their very nature mean that people doing them see-saw between the anxiety of demand and the relief of meeting that demand. A journalist told us:

> It's a lot of pressure, a lot of rushing around, bad diet, fast food, odd times when you have a bit too much to drink, ridiculous hours, jumping when telephones go off. Even when you're not working and the telephone goes at home – boom, it sort of kicks into you. But I don't think I could ever do a nine to five. It would just become so tedious, too boring, too normal. But in the middle of it you can suddenly stop when a story has been racing along and then you've filed and that's it for the day. And you wind down completely. And you'll go off and have some fun or something like that and then the next development you're immediately

hiked up again and away you go. It's constantly on and off all the time.

Fleet Street [is] like, you know, a very demanding mistress – once you get hooked on it you're gone. It's crazy. It's like a drug.

Unfortunately, this addictive quality of noradrenalin can be dangerous at two levels: firstly, because it keeps people in stressful jobs and positions in which their arousal levels are consistently raised and, secondly, because even noradrenalin if constantly present in the bloodstream has detrimental effects on the vascular system. We discuss this effect in more detail in a later chapter.

It's clear that extended, acute periods of stress produce a wide variety of physical illnesses simply because we are not designed to stay in the distressed physiological state that's produced by both adrenalin and noradrenalin for any length of time.

How stress affects our minds

I went for the booze and the pills, Christmas Eve, you know, you've got to be pretty far down to do that. I kept going to work, but I was on anti-depressants and that, so I was spaced out all the time, I didn't have any feelings at all. I was completely numb, and you know, I just didn't care, I'd just had enough.

I was what they call withdrawn ... and I couldn't hardly speak to anybody. I was spending a lot of time on me own, and I couldn't stand having anybody near me or anything. I was really, you know, pretty down and ... I was frightened that I was going to be locked up and the key thrown away. I literally thought they were going to put me into an institution. (Hospital porter)

It's been estimated that about 15 per cent of the whole population suffer from some kind of psychological symptoms of stress at some time in their lives, and much of this can be accounted for by problems they have at work. But the conscious experience of mental stress is complicated to account for. Detailed work by Jeffrey Gray and his colleagues at Oxford University has suggested that there are almost certainly risk-monitoring devices built directly into our brains, and that we share these devices with all other animals down to the humble goldfish.

When the perceived probability of danger increases beyond a certain point, anxiety is produced. It seems likely that we can also be made anxious when we have to attempt to act correctly in ambiguous situations or to control uncontrollable events, or simply when we find it difficult to adjust to a particular situation. We can be depressed both by attempting to deal with too much information, or by not having enough information to deal with. Depression also often results from a major shock or bereavement, and simply attempting to cope with continuing change seems to use up some mental capacity to adapt, often resulting in depression. People also inherit from their parents greater or lesser mental vulnerability to stress, and some seem to have been affected by early life events.

If workers are not able to cope with feelings of anxiety or depression they may well display a range of symptoms which tend to resemble exaggerated or distorted forms of otherwise normal personality characteristics which they already possess. Thus an isolated kind of person may show signs of paranoia and a fear of others conspiring against him, a careful person may become obsessional, and so on. Sometimes the symptoms produced can be downright bizzare and deeply worrying to the person concerned.

A secretary described her symptoms when she finally collapsed after a long period of overwork operating a word processor.

I was very confused when I became ill. I was disorientated – spatially disorientated. My whole spatial sense had gone. I couldn't walk properly. And I was terrified. Terrified of lots of things. For instance, several months before I became ill one of the symptoms leading up to it was that if anybody stood on the left-hand side of me, I felt terrified in the left-hand side of my body! And I would have to ask people to stand on the other side of me. And then I didn't feel frightened if they stood there. And I worked at an L-shaped desk, with the word processor and the VDU unit on my left and my papers on my right, so the part of me that was exposed mostly to the machine I hated was my left-hand side. I mean, one tries to rationalise the reason for these things.

Here's a list of the most common mental symptoms of stress, If you'd like to check your own stress level, answer Yes if you've experienced these feelings regularly or are experiencing them now.

Mental symptoms of stress

* I feel angry all the time.
* I have lost interest in sex.
* I can't make up my mind, and often feel I can't cope.
* I feel like a failure.
* No one likes me or cares about me.
* I don't like other people or myself very much.
* I fear something dreadful will happen.
* I can't concentrate and often find it hard to complete a task before going on to the next.
* I can't tell other people how I feel.
* I've lost my sense of humour and can't take an interest in life.

If you've answered Yes to more than 5 of the questions, you are probably experiencing stress at a level that could ultimately damage your health, but don't worry *too* much. Human beings have an enormous capacity to regenerate their mental and physical health and happiness, and a valuable first step is just checking yourself against this list. If you are experiencing these feelings now you are not unique or alone and you are certainly not going crazy. Understanding the source of your problems is halfway to beating them.

How stress affects our behaviour

People find it difficult to cope in different ways. Some sort of react to the pressure by keeping their heads down all day working flat out as if they're working in a factory, but skimming over the top of the work. Some people it affects totally in the way they just sit back and think, Well it's too much for me to cope with so I won't even both trying to start.

I can think of particular instances of people who started drinking heavily. I mean, there's one of my best friends who actually has a serious drink problem, due I think at least partly to work. (Tax officer)

Stress at work can be revealed by a number of well recognised behaviour patterns, including absenteeism, lateness, high labour turnover, strikes, disputes and even physical violence. A production-line worker described what can happen when the pressure rises:

I know people who freak out by just coming in, clocking out and going home. .... People react in all different ways because of the pressure. When it becomes intense they just blow up, in other words fly off the handle. I've seen a bloke hit a foreman for no apparent reason . . . he was just asking him about his job – something that he does every day – and he just turned around and smacked him.

But the symptoms are not always as straightforward as this. When experiencing mental stress, people often try to cope in various ways. Some of their attempts will produce effective action, but others are simply well established psychological mechanisms by which people attempt to trick themselves into avoiding or denying their stress. The most common ones are the following:

Displacement. Under stress, aggression is often displaced by people from the true cause of their frustration, which they feel they can't attack – for example, the boss – on to someone whom they feel they can attack – the spouse at home, or the people subordinate to them at work. One young tax officer put it this way: 'I try to cope by trying to leave the job behind when I go home. I used to be able to do it. I used to come in and do my job and go home and shut the door and forget it. I find I can't do that any more. I take it home with me. I take the stress home with me, I shout at my husband.'

Nostalgia, fantasy and play. Groups of workers who find themselves trapped into static or boring jobs often spend a lot of time either talking about 'the good old days', daydreaming about what they might do when they are out of the work situation, or larking about when supervisors are away.

An electronics assembly worker described a typical day at work: 'I just think what I'm going to do at night, how drunk I'm going to get at the weekend, basic things like that, what I've got to do to my scooter. I never think about me work 'cos there's nothing to think about – your mind sort of goes numb.' And a production-line worker said: 'That's how most people spend their lives in there – just wishing their life away inside the factory, waiting until the final bell goes.'

Apathy. Following an initial period of effort and struggle without sufficient reward, some workers (especially those who feel themselves on a career plateau, for example in middle age) often simply give in. They adopt behaviour patterns like coming in as late as possible, minimising their contact with other workers, and devising techniques for meeting the stated demands of the job without having to engage their own drive or commitment.

In addition, many people working in the caring professions (like nurses or social workers), faced with the irreconcilable divide between the job they are trained to do and the real facilities and conditions under which they have to work, may succumb to what's been described as emotional burnout, another apathetic state which we discuss more fully later in the book.

One social worker described how she felt: 'The job was draining all the energy I had, was being drained into getting nowhere at work. So there was precious little left. And when I got home I just slept, and was irritable. Not to the flaming rows state, but I just had to batten myself down, there was nothing left to give.'

Specialisation. Almost the mirror image of apathy as a coping device for escaping stress, 'specialisation' is when individuals throw themselves into one particular aspect of their work in order to forget the more unpleasant aspects of their job situation.

This technique has been recognised in people who have to do jobs about which they personally may feel some moral ambiguity – such as being a tabloid journalist or a soldier or a prison officer. In this situation people may become obsessed with career advancement or professional 'style'. Alternatively, workers in more conventional industries who are stressed and frustrated and feel their abilities are not recognised may throw themselves wholeheartedly into union and social activities.

Denial. Some workers under stress may simply deny the fact of their stress altogether, instead producing individual physical symptoms or indeed mass illnesses where a whole factory population may unconsciously decide that they've all developed the same minor illness.

Mass psychogenic illnesses have been identified several times in America, though not so far in this country. What happens is that employees in an electronics assembly plant, or an aluminium assembly plant or a shoe factory, suddenly and collectively complain of headaches, nausea, nasty tastes in their mouths or bad smells. On investigation, no physical cause for these symptoms can be found, but these outbreaks have always been revealed to have been precipitated by widespread physical and psychological stress in the particular workplace.

Addictions and distractions. Finally, smoking, drinking excessive amounts of alcohol, overeating and even adultery have all been recognised as coping mechanisms used to avoid the awareness of work stress.

Smoking is one of the commonest ways of dealing with stress, as one businessman found. 'I perhaps smoked about thirty cigarettes a day, and the pressure point would come if I'd got a difficult telephone conversation. I would never answer the phone unless I got a cigarette, and that was probably one of these habits that you acquire over a period of time, but since my heart attack I've stopped smoking.'

Women are also showing more signs of 'stress-coping behaviour' like smoking and heavy drinking. Bobby Jacobson in her recent book, *The Lady Killers: Why Smoking is a Feminist Issue*, noted that female managers in the United States now smoke more than their male counterparts; 42 per cent of women executives smoke regularly as against only 30 per cent of men in similar jobs. By the end of the 1970s more than 8500 women died from lung cancer every year in the States, and Jacobson found that there was a direct link between the increase in women smoking and their appearance in the full-time labour force.

In a recent British study, 74 per cent of women who smoked claimed they did so because of work stress. Since 65 per cent of all women between the ages of 16 and 59 in Britain now work, their experience in the workplace will undoubtedly play an increasing part in their physical and emotional well-being.

Stress and particular illnesses

> I knew that something was going to happen to me, because when I left the office, at around seven, I really did feel in quite a state. I'd got myself wound up, I know that, I thought that somehow I'd got to calm myself down, but driving back from the office I felt my arms go on the steering wheel and something was obviously going wrong.
>
> I can't recall a lot about it, except that I was lying in a hospital wired up to various things, thinking, Oh dear, what's going to happen now. I was taken home and I think I'd been home around ten days – I'd had quite a serious heart attack and . . . I had another one, lying in bed. . . . I thought, well at the age of forty-nine I've had two heart attacks, and this really is going to be a very difficult period because a lot of my friends had had them. Some had survived, in this rat race we are involved in, but it became pretty obvious that I was not going to be able to cope with what I'd coped with previously. (Former general manager)

The stress symptoms seem to be a sign that our bodies are in the process of responding to extended demand of some kind, but predicting exactly what form of illness that might ultimately produce is more difficult.

It's now widely accepted that virtually all illnesses have some psychosomatic component. Later in this book we'll look in more detail at Holmes and Rahe's famous Life Event Scale, which tries to assess just how much impact different events have on people's health. Often people become ill as a response to a single event like a divorce, bereavement or being dismissed from work. At first sight this seems to contradict our understanding of stress illness as the ultimate result of extended demands on our adaptive capacity, but it's a bit more complicated than that.

In 1963 Dr David Kissen carried out a major study of sick Glaswegian industrial workers which revealed a clear link between developing lung cancer and being the kind of person who doesn't express their feelings. Subsequent follow-up studies which still continue have made this link more and more clear. Two American researchers, R. L. Horne and R. S. Picard, claim that by using more subtle personality tests, developed from those first used by Kissen, they can predict with 73 per cent accuracy whether a person suffering from respiratory disease does in fact have cancer.

It seems that some people, through their inability to express and perhaps relieve their feelings, have particular difficulty in coping with shocks and challenges. This can be reflected in the extended periods of depression and mourning which often come before the onset of lung cancer. Similar personality traits have also been found among many bereaved women who ultimately suffer from breast cancer.

Heart attacks have a well-established commonsense link with being rushed and aggressive at work. This seems to be related to a number of changes in the blood chemistry of people of a certain temperament, who stress themselves by constantly taking on enormous amounts of work. This stress is reflected not only in their blood fat and blood sugar levels, but in the overproduction of the hormones adrenalin and noradrenalin, and we will discuss new research in this area in more detail in Chapter Three.

It is worth noting that the incidence of heart attacks is rising in the UK at a time when it is falling in many other countries in the West, and no one is precisely sure why this is happening. In England and Wales, for example, the death rate amongst men between the ages of 35 and 44 doubled during the years between 1950 and 1973, and this was a much more rapid increase than that amongst older men of between 45 and 54. Over 40 per cent of all deaths among younger men were due to some form of cardiovascular disease.

It has been argued that the dramatic drop in heart attacks – about 27 per cent – amongst American males aged between 40 to 69 over the last ten years reflects the growing popular concern in the United States with physical fitness and diet. It may well be that their increasing awareness of the reality of stress as a source of illness, reflected in the growth of corporate health schemes, is also a factor in this reduction. Certainly, improved diet can't be the whole answer. It has been shown that, even with a zero intake of cholesterol, people's blood cholesterol levels are only reduced by about 16 per cent. Stress is therefore clearly a major factor in heart disease.

Professor Cary Cooper believes that the dramatic World Health Organisation figures on pages 19 and 20 reflect not only changes in diet in the countries where heart disease is declining, but a decrease in work and home stress levels generally. He believes that active stress reduction programmes involving physical exercise, cutting down smoking and alcohol, and stress management, are a major factor in reducing illness in the countries where employers have initiated them.

As well as being implicated in the development of circulatory and heart diseases and some forms of cancer, stress has also been suggested as a major contributory factor in a number of other illnesses – including diabetes, rheumatism and arthritis, various allergies and skin diseases, asthma, multiple sclerosis, ulcers and other stomach complaints. It has also been suggested that stress can act as a precipitating factor in the onset of almost any major illness including many of those which we're used to thinking of as being the direct result of infection. The key to this relationship seems to lie in the effect of stress on the auto-immune or self-defence system of the body.

The auto-immune system in stress

We are constantly encountering agencies and infections which could potentially render us ill, but we are protected from them most of the time by the auto-immune system. This system has two main arms each depending mainly on defence cells called lymphocytes.

**Average increase/decrease in mortality from
ischaemic heart disease 1968–1977 (40–69 age group)**

Men

	Decrease		*Increase*
USA	−27%	Scotland	+ 1%
Japan	−25%	England and Wales	+ 3%
Austria	−20%	Northern Ireland	+12%
Finland	−18%	Ireland	+30%
Norway	−11%	Hungary	
Holland	−10%	Poland	
Italy	− 2%	Rumania	over 30%
		Bulgaria	
		Yugoslavia	

(Source: WHO 1982)

Deaths per 100,000
(40–69 age group)

Men

Finland	673
Scotland	615
Northern Ireland	614
USA	528
Ireland	508
England and Wales	498
West Germany	325
Bulgaria	237
Poland	229
France	152
Japan	69

(Source: WHO 1982)

The first arm of this system depends for the most part on
what are called T-cell leucocytes, which are produced by the
thymus gland in our chests. The leucocytes stimulate the white
blood cells and themselves literally attack and destroy infecting
micro-organisms. They also neutralise the effects of carcenogenic
agencies like ultra-violet rays and toxic chemicals. They do this
by producing a number of substances called lymphokines, and
one of these is the famous anti-cancer substance Interferon. It
has been estimated that roughly half the body's total defences

**Average increase/decrease in mortality from
ischaemic heart disease 1968–1977 (40–69 age group)**

Women

	Decrease		*Increase*
Japan	−39%	Scotland	+10%
USA	−31%	England and Wales	+11%
Italy	−20%	Hungary	
Finland	−15%	Poland	
France	−14%	Rumania	over 20%
Norway	−2%	Bulgaria	
Northern Ireland	0	Yugoslavia	

(Source: WHO 1982)

**Deaths per 100,000
(40–69 age group)**

Women

Scotland	202
Israel	193
Northern Ireland	189
USA	171
Ireland	168
Finland	142
England and Wales	138
Bulgaria	110
West Germany	84
Italy	63
France	37
Japan	29

(Source: WHO 1982)

come from this arm of the system.

The other arm depends on the less direct action of a group of cells called B-cell lymphocytes. These produce specific antibodies against infections, neutralise foreign anti-gens, and make it easier for white blood cells to destroy invaders by coating the cells of the invader. It seems to be the case that the adrenalin released during stress provokes the production of lymphocytes by *challenging* the immune system. In the process it may actually *inhibit* the action of the white blood cells which are the rank-and-file army of defenders against infection or cancer-producing cells. The corticosteroid messengers which stimulate the hippocampus as part of the stress response also inhibit the action of protective lymphocytes as well as that of the macrophages, the giant killer cells which literally swallow up and destroy foreign cells.

It appears that the depression and repressed emotion of the shocked or bereaved may facilitate the development of cancer by increasing the production of corticosteroids which in turn repress the function of the immune system. It also seems likely that many other illnesses, from which we are normally protected, are able to take hold as a secondary effect of stress, depending on particular conditions and our own particular inherited constitution.

The scale of stress illness

It's very difficult to evaluate precisely how much impact stress – and job stress in particular – has on our health as a nation, though a number of observers believe that the general level of stress is high and increasing. It was pointed out in a review of the effects of stress in *The Times* in 1983 that about 30 million working days were officially lost each year due to nervous ailments often associated with stress. The government assessment of public health in 1978, published by HMSO, estimated that about 5 million people (10.9 per cent of the population) consulted their doctor each year about mental health problems, and 600,000 (1.3 per cent) used specific psychiatric services. More young people complain of mental symptoms every year.

However, many other short-term mental and behavioural symptoms of stress are probably euphemised as colds, headaches or flu when reported to doctors. Similarly, a vast proportion of the ulcers, high blood pressure, rheumatism and migraines reported to doctors must be exacerbated, if not directly caused, by stress. This has been estimated at perhaps another 25 million working days lost. Another difficulty in tracing the actual scale of stress illness is due to the different ways in which different groups of people experience and report their illness. Many working-class people expect aches and pains, headaches and stomach upsets to increase with age and do not report these to anyone medically qualified. People suffering from mental illness which is intensifying the effect of physical symptoms will often present these alone to the doctor, and not mention their anxiety and depression. Most people still don't associate their problems at work with the physical and mental symptoms they experience, and many doctors will still ask about these background factors in only the most casual way.

Taking all these factors into account, it seems safe to say that at least 40 million working days are lost in Britain each year due directly to the effects of stress, and this adds at least £55m of direct costs to the medical and social services and loses us 2 to 3 per cent of the GNP each year.

Positive stress?

We said at the beginning of this chapter that it's important to be clear that if we restrict our definition of stress to those demands which actually make people *ill*. Many work situations which we might *assume* are stressful are actually not. Many jobs make high demands on their practitioners and require them to work at high arousal levels, but by no means all the people in these professions become ill and many seem actively to thrive on demanding jobs.

How does this fit our picture of the way that continued high arousal can make us ill? The stimulation and interest that goes with meeting a challenging task has been called 'positive stress', but this is actually a contradiction in terms. It also confuses people when they are trying to assess whether or not they should modify their own behaviour at work.

The key to understanding why excitement and demand makes us ill in some situations but stimulates and energises us in others lies in the vital role our own perception of the situation has in influencing our body chemistry. For our TV series we carried out an experiment with the help of Dr Malcolm Carruthers of the Positive Health Centre in London. Recently Dr Carruthers and his colleagues have set up a mobile stress detection laboratory with which he can visit a particular firm, carry out confidential blood tests and questionnaires on all its employees and, by analysing the samples on the spot, warn those who are in danger from stress and offer them specific advice on what sort of action they might take to relieve it. The test equipment requires just a tiny drop of blood to carry out the analysis and this helps people to accept the idea of giving blood. The procedure is, as Dr Carruthers puts it, 'finger prickin' good'!

We took his laboratory along to a motor rally circuit at Sunningdale, where three experienced rally drivers were to compete in time trials against one another, over a rough cross-country course. Dr Carruthers took blood samples from each driver before the race started. He analysed this blood and noted the blood levels of free fatty acids and tryglycerides, which indicate how much noradrenalin is circulating in the bloodstream. He also analysed the levels of glucose and lactates, which indicate adrenalin and the levels of cortisol. He also measured heart rate. The three men varied in their anxiety levels before the race. Two of them were older and more experienced and this was reflected in their more positive attitude, although their blood chemistry was broadly similar. For all three men their heart rates rose to around 140 just before the race and their heart rates were still in the 120s when the race was over, which demonstrates how rapidly and dramatically people's blood rate and pressure rises in response to arousal.

The most interesting aspect of their physiological state, however, was the way their blood chemistry changed after the race. As it happened, the two losers came in with identical times and, by coincidence, these were the two older and more confident men. Both men showed slightly raised levels of noradrenalin, reflecting the physical effort they had made and their interests in the race, but they also showed higher levels of adrenalin and raised blood cortisol. The winner, on the other hand, showed raised levels of noradrenalin but his cortisol levels were *down*.

Our little experiment broadly confirmed the results of several other surveys and experiments. Together they suggest that our *appraisal* of events as either threatening and potentially negative, or challenging and positive, can act directly to influence our blood chemistry. These blood chemistry changes will in turn directly affect our health.

In one Swedish study at a wood-processing plant the researchers gave volunteers two kinds of job to do – one that they could easily control and which they found challenging, and one over which they had no control. As their blood was analysed it was seen that adrenalin levels went up for both jobs which reflected the demand made on them. But blood cortisol levels fell in the people who were doing the job which they found challenging but controllable.

So the picture is more complicated than just making a simple distinction between positive and negative stress. What actually happens is that both adrenalin and noradrenalin levels are raised in our bloodstreams in response to effort and involvement, but this only becomes damaging if it's consistent and unremitting arousal over a period of time. More damaging are raised levels of adrenalin and lowered levels of cortisol, which are associated with feelings of threat or defeat and which produce lowered immune function. However, the cortisol level in our bloodstream also goes down during periods of variety and stimulating challenge, together with a positive attitude to events, and there is an increasing amount of evidence that people who are able to feel positive about what they do, and what happens to them, are in some way actively protected *against* ill health. We discuss this at more length in Chapter Three.

Of course, one major element in our appraisal of the work situation is the actual reality of it. If we are consistently attempting to cope with truly impossible demands, to control uncontrollable situations or cope with threats of social rejection or dismissal at work, then the job that we have to do can be directly blamed for the destructive stress it produces.

On the other hand, if we find our job satisfying and sustaining, we can similarly attribute a lot of our positive feelings (and health) to the job itself. So the next thing to sort out is what makes a particular job stressful or satisfying? And which *are* the best and worst jobs?

CHAPTER TWO

Job satisfaction

Trying to understand why different jobs stress or satisfy the people who do them is made more difficult by the fact that, as a society, we're very ambivalent about the idea of working generally. We inherit attitudes to work which were drawn from the times when many people were obliged to labour from dawn to dusk, first in the fields and then more recently in mills and factories, just to survive.

Both employers and unions have come to see labour as a commodity, something that costs each individual worker his effort, and therefore something that should cost each employer money. All jobs are demanding in some way, and many people still understand stress to be simply some form of excessive demand. As a result, many employers still feel that their workers really shouldn't complain about sometimes having to make excessive efforts, because effort is just what they're buying from them and companies often specify 'the ability to work under pressure' as a job qualification. The trade unions don't seem to take job stress very seriously either. The issue isn't even mentioned in the 176-page TUC handbook on health at work.

It is true that there have been major initiatives on work-stress policy from one or two big unions – for example, ASTMS and APEX. ASTMS would like to see British companies introduce more American-style stress-reduction programmes, and see jobs designed to exert less pressure on workers. However, most unions and their health officers still tend to be more worried about physical stress factors like noise, and new equipment, than the more intangible issues of workers' involvement in planning, or the regulation of the pace at which they work. Indeed, many trade unionists are still deeply suspicious of the *idea* of job-stress at all, insofar as they see it as a sneaky attempt to involve workers in the task of reorganising employment, which they believe is actually the responsibility of managers and employers.

Still, alongside this widespread belief that work must, by its very nature, in some way be demanding and uncomfortable, it's also widely recognised in our society that being employed can be a source of deep satisfaction. It ties us to reality, providing each worker with a great deal of the sense of purpose and meaning in their lives, and sometimes all of it. In one survey, in 1976, people were asked 'If you won £250,000 on the pools would you carry on with your present job?' More than half of them said that they would.

Intelligent employers have long understood that there are considerable gains for them, even in the most material sense, if their employees are happy at their work. Workplaces where people describe themselves as satisfied with their jobs tend to have low levels of accidents, lateness, absenteeism, and labour turnover, as well as producing fewer below-standard goods, and fewer strikes and disputes. However, research by industrial psychologists established as early as the 1940s that just because people felt more satisfied with their jobs, didn't mean that they were necessarily more productive in them. And this finding still turns up in more recent studies of job satisfaction.

For a while during the fifties and sixties, employer interest in the idea of job satisfaction lay fallow, although social and industrial psychologists continued to investigate the various sources of job satisfaction. Their findings were undoubtedly taken into account by a minority of progressive and liberal managers working in the middle ground between employers and labour. Firms like Marks and Spencers, United Biscuits and the John Lewis Partnership established a reputation for employee care which is still maintained.

During the late seventies and early eighties, however, as the connection between stress and illness and death moved from suspicion to a certainty, it has clearly become a matter of urgent concern to understand why people are happy or unhappy at work, how this relates to stress-related illness and then to put these findings into practice.

In recent times, it's become clear that being *un*employed can also have very destructive effects, not only on the financial well-being of the unemployed, but on their physical and mental health. It seems logical that this should be so. Being unemployed cuts people off from many of the vital sources of satisfaction that are usually provided by their job. If, as is widely believed, many of the people who are now out of work will never be fully employed again – with many more of us due to join them – it becomes even more vital for researchers to try to abstract the sources of job satisfaction in employment. We must see if they can't in some way be separated from the actual process of being employed, and offered to people *not* in work.

Job satisfaction versus stress?

It seems likely that people who are happy and satisfied at work are probably going to be less stressed than those who are dissatisfied. So what are the crucial aspects of the jobs that we do that make them either satisfactory or unsatisfactory? As a rule of thumb, if someone says they are satisfied with one main aspect of their job, then they tend to be satisfied with all of it. One survey done in America in the late 1940s asked workers first of all to identify what were the chief sources of satisfaction in their job, and then to rank them in order of importance. The list came out like this: security, the prospect of promotion, interesting work, the company worked for, rates of pay, behaviour of co-workers, the behaviour of supervisors, working hours and working conditions. This seems a straightforward and plausible list, but of course it doesn't differentiate between different sorts of people in different sorts of jobs.

A few years ago *Which?* magazine carried out a useful survey of 24,000 of its readers by asking them the same kind of questions. Top of the list of job satisfactions came 'use made of my abilities' and, next, 'interest in the work I do'. *Which?* went on to tie their list to specific aspects of their readers' jobs, like the size of firm they worked for, or their position in it. From this they built up a detailed and interesting picture of just what kind of job satisfied most of their readers best.

Apparently, the most satisfied workers tended to be employed by a small firm, where they had a responsible position, worked long hours and had lots to do, had some control over what they did and felt their work was important and mattered to the firm. They usually had some kind of professional qualification and they were better paid than average. In fact, 90 per cent of *Which?*'s correspondents who fitted this picture said they were either satisfied or very satisfied with their particular job. Once again, however, physical working conditions and hours worked were the least important elements in the job satisfaction lists of most correspondents. This might of course have simply reflected the fact that the *Which?* sample was heavily biased towards the

---

Which job?

Here's how the different jobs were rated in reply to *Which?*'s main question about job satisfaction:

Overall, how satisfied are you with your present job?

More than averagely satisfied	% very satisfied	Less than averagely satisfied	% very satisfied
clergyman	58	economist	19
company director	48	computer programmer/ systems analyst	18
farmer/horticulturalist	48	laboratory assistant	18
optician	45	skilled manual jobs (e.g. engineer, printer, welder)	18
solicitor/barrister	43		
primary school teacher	42		
shopkeeper	42	engineer (all professional types, including civil, electrical, electronic and mechanical)	17
university/polytechnic teacher	41		
photographer/ cameraman	39	secretarial and clerical jobs (e.g. secretary, typist, telephonist)	17
insurance broker	37	management trainee	16
vet	37		
actor/musician	36	unskilled manual jobs (e.g. building labourer, shop assistant)	15
social worker/ probation officer	35		
		market researcher	14
		research officer/ assistant	14
		actuary	11
		draughtsman	8

(From *Which?*, 'How you rate your jobs', September 1977)

jobs and interests of its largely middle-class readership; however, a sufficiently large number of different occupations were represented for *Which?* to feel that they could make a list of jobs in order of high to low job satisfaction.

Which? noted that most of the jobs that were high on the job satisfaction list seemed to be those where people had a higher than average degree of control over how they did the job, and that many of these were professional and vocational jobs. When they asked people which aspects of their job they were *least* satisfied with, 54 per cent were unhappy with the way the organisation was run, about a half were dissatisfied with their pay, about a third with chances of promotion, and one third just didn't like the person they worked for.

Here's a list of fifteen of the most important sources of satisfaction or dissatisfaction which people describe at work. Answer Yes or No for each item according to your feelings about that particular aspect of your job. Are you satisfied or dissatisfied with:

1 The physical work conditions
2 Your colleagues
3 Your salary
4 Industrial relations between management and staff
5 Your hours of work
6 The freedom to choose your own method of working
7 The recognition you get for good work
8 Your immediate boss
9 The way you are managed
10 The attention paid to the suggestions you make
11 The amount of responsibility you are given
12 The opportunity to use your abilities
13 The amount of variety in your job
14 Your chance of promotion
15 Your job security

If you are dissatisfied with more than 8 items then you join about one third of all British workers who when tested in this way describe themselves as largely dissatisfied with their jobs.

However, does this mean that you're more *stressed*? In the

last few years, interest in job satisfaction has been more urgently replaced by a concern for the stress rating of different jobs, and in 1984 a *Sunday Times* survey of job opportunities for young people offered a stress rating for each profession described. This was drawn up by Professor Cary Cooper, and to do this he averaged the stress assessments of six different academic researchers. Subsequently he drew all these ratings together into the list below. Even a fairly casual comparison of the two lists – *Which?*'s satisfaction list and Cooper's stress list – makes it clear that job stress and job dissatisfaction are not necessarily quite the same thing.

The stress rate is from 10 to nil. The higher your rating the greater the stress.

Profession	Rating	Profession	Rating	Profession	Rating
Miner	8.3	Press officer	5.8	Town hall staff	4.3
Police	7.7	Professional		Artist, designer	4.2
Airline pilot	7.5	footballer	5.8	Architect	4.0
Building worker	7.5	Salesman, shop		Chiropodist	4.0
Journalist	7.5	assistant	5.7	Optician	4.0
Prison officer	7.5	Stockbroker	5.5	Planner	4.0
Advertising	7.3	Bus driver	5.4	Postman	4.0
Dentist	7.3	Psychologist	5.2	Statistcan	4.0
Actor	7.2	Publisher	5.0	Lab technician	3.8
Politician	7.0	Diplomat	4.8	Banker	3.7
Doctor	6.8	Farmer	4.8	Computing	3.7
Taxman	6.8	Armed forces	4.7	Linguist	3.7
Film producer	6.5	Vet	4.5	Occupational	
Nurse, midwife	6.5	Civil servant	4.4	therapist	3.7
Fireman	6.3	Accountant	4.3	Beauty therapist	3.5
Pop musician	6.3	Engineer	4.3	Vicar	3.5
Teacher	6.2	Estate agent	4.3	Astronomer	3.4
Personnel	6.0	Hairdresser	4.3	Nursery nurse	3.3
Social worker	6.0	Secretary	4.3	Museum worker	2.8
Manager	5.8	Solicitor	4.3	Librarian	2.0

Clergymen, for example, are very high on the job satisfaction list and very low on the stress list, which seems to make sense, and building labourers are low on job satisfaction and high on stress, which you might expect, but many professions like actors, musicians, teachers, and social workers were high on both lists.

It has been suggested that the weakness of trying to use people's description of job satisfaction as a direct predictor of job stress, is because it depends on a rather one-dimensional way of looking at satisfaction.

The idea has been put forward by Peter Warr at Sheffield University that people's experience of work varies not only according to how much they enjoy what they are doing, but also how much it arouses them physiologically. If you take these two dimensions – arousal and enjoyment – into account, this seems to make slightly more sense of the disparities between the two lists. If someone describes themselves as feeling contented but made aroused by their job, you might expect them to feel energised but cheerful, and therefore not particularly stressed. If they're discontented, but at low arousal, they may feel sad or even depressed – but not necessarily stressed. And certainly, if they feel contented and at low arousal, then they simply feel relaxed. But if they feel discontented *and* aroused, then they will feel anxious, and anxiety is strongly correlated with stress.

Still, anxiety of itself is not the same thing as stress, and we shouldn't assume that simply because someone's job sometimes makes them aroused and anxious, that they will necessarily suffer from stress, or low mental health. To become damaging, anxiety has to be severe, extended and inappropriate. This is reflected in the fact that, for example, some air-traffic controllers who have to do a notoriously demanding job may well show anxious personality characteristics, yet suffer from no more frequent mental and physical ill-health than their more equable colleagues. However, air-traffic controllers who are poor at social skills and don't feel themselves supported by the people they work with, do have higher than average levels of illness. And this reflects the importance of social support in counteracting job stress.

The picture's even more complicated than that, however. Although it's generally true that stress, as revealed by illness, tends to decrease as job status and skill level rise, we still find many people in demanding supervisory jobs who, although they report themselves as being happy and satisfied with the job they do, still display a variety of psychosomatic illnesses.

The extent to which our job requires or invites us to maintain a constant high level of arousal is one major factor in the extent to which it predisposes us to physical illness. Although feeling contented or discontented with our job may be an important factor in our subjective experience of it, it doesn't coincide exactly with the extent to which the job may be actually damaging us.

It has been argued that a 'stress league' of jobs is meaningless because the extent to which a particular job stresses you will depend on your own personality and how well suited and happy you are with your particular position and employers. Personality is certainly a vital part of the job stress picture, and we discuss it in the next chapter, but it isn't all of it. This is clearly revealed by the pattern of illnesses and deaths among different parts of the working population.

Industrial death rate league chart

The tables below show the death rate per 1000 of men aged 15–64 in different occupations

High death rate		*Low death rate*	
Coal miners (underground)	8.22	University teachers	2.87
Shoemakers, and shoe repairers	8.98	Physiotherapists	2.97
		Paper products makers	3.02
Leather products makers	8.95	Managers in building and contracting	3.19
Machine tool operators	9.14		
Watch repairers	9.46	Local authority senior officers	3.42
Coal miners (above ground)	9.72		
Steel erectors, riggers	9.92	Ministers of the Crown, MPs, senior government officials	3.71
Fishermen	10.28		
Labourers and unskilled workers, all industries	12.47	Primary and secondary school teachers	3.96
Policemen	12.70	Sales managers	4.21
Bricklayers' labourers	16.44	Architects, town planners	4.43
Electrical engineers	19.04	Civil service executive officers	4.67
		Postmen	4.84
		Medical practitioners	4.94

(Source: Black, 1980 and *The Sunday Times*, 21 August 1980)

Once again the picture is complicated because death rates do not of course exactly mirror stress rates and, as you might expect, the death-rate league chart shown here doesn't exactly fit either of our two previous lists. This follows from the fact that different jobs present different kinds of stresses and that different groups of workers react to them in different ways.

In general, manual workers die more often and at a younger age than white-collar staff. The unskilled develop and die more often from cancer, heart failure and chest diseases. Incidentally, the wives and families of manual workers suffer more from stress-related illnesses than do those of white-collar workers and, in a series of fascinating researches, the psychologist Ben Fletcher has revealed that the *pattern* of illness suffered by spouses often mirrors that of their working partner. Thus wives of miners suffer from bronchial illness more often then average and those of stressed executives more often from heart attacks.

It's widely believed that heart attacks are the favourite stress ailment of high-ranking executives and that this group suffers abnormally from cardiovascular diseases compared to other workers. In fact, *middle* managers have 40 per cent more heart attacks than top executives, and one famous American study revealed that, in one company at least, skilled manual workers suffered two and a half times more heart attacks than all managers. What *is* true is that a certain kind of heart-attack-prone personality often turns up amongst ambitious, go-getting executives (and we discuss this in more detail later) but the managerial classes don't have a monopoly of this type of personality.

Manual workers are far more likely to encounter physical stressors like noise, heat and chemical fumes, along with demanding physical effort and changing shift-times. They are also more likely to suffer from accidents. Shift-workers tend to suffer more gastro-intestinal diseases and more serious accidents. For all workers, changes in temperature and vibration have been shown to affect blood circulation and heart function.

It's been observed that, in general, manual workers tend to react with more physical symptoms of stress, and white-collar workers with more mental symptoms, but this is a very wide generalisation. Certainly the mental stresses of many clerical and managerial jobs are quite different from those of manual jobs, as we will see later in this book.

However, the specific stresses of each job vary a great deal, as has been revealed by the now vast numbers of stress studies of particular occupations, and the increasing tendency of groups of workers – including one-man train and bus drivers, post-office workers, teachers, social workers, tax officers, policemen and a wide range of clerical and manual working groups – to complain and campaign about the stresses of their job. Stress has even been made the central issue in a number of industrial disputes.

Each job has its own particular task specifications and demands. Taking a selection of high stress jobs almost at random: even moderately senior banking staff have a great deal of personal responsibility for the loans they arrange, the customers they arrange them with and the terms and conditions of repayment. But they have to operate between the demands of their not always trustworthy clients and the watchful eye of their superiors who demand that they observe the most rigid and proper procedures. Conflict between demands is a typical stressor for many dentists. They are trained to save teeth and help people, but in practice they often have to remove teeth and often can't help hurting people. They also tend to feel lonely and isolated.

Air-traffic controllers notoriously suffer from the stress illnesses, particularly heart attacks, associated with a highly responsible task where important and far-reaching decisions have to be made immediately. Farmers, on the other hand, have to invest and plan for long periods ahead when not only the market, but the complex government system of checks and subsidies may alter abruptly. All these jobs have above average physical and mental stress symptom rates, including, for some of them, death by suicide. But the list goes on and on. One-man bus drivers often feel, like the growing army of word-processor and VDU operators, that they are simply extensions of a machine. Aeroplane pilots (predominately male), on the other hand, are often stressed by the need to cope with all the problems and worries of the rest of the crew, plus their own erratic home lives – now often complicated by the fact that their wives increasingly have their own careers to think about.

We discuss the particular problems of these and several other groups of workers in more detail throughout the rest of this book, but just to list and describe the ways in which particular jobs have particularly stressing job-specifications is clearly not enough. Not only does each occupation have its own particular task specifications and demands, but each job also varies in the extent to which the individuals who do it are required to react to *change* (itself a major source of stress). Some occupations involve complicated career development adjustments to promotion, demotion or just plain old career plateaus. In others, workers have to adapt constantly to technological changes and changing job demands. These problems are often encountered by several different kinds of workers in the new hi-tech industries – for example, in the development, making and selling of hi-tech products. Different professions are also differently vulnerable to changes in the wider society; these include changes in government policy and cuts in the finance of state-run services, the collapse of the older, heavy 'primary' industries, or just changes in the general pattern of employment – as for example in the way that women are now replacing men, not only in manual and service jobs but with increasing frequency in executive and managerial positions.

However, not *everyone* who carries out a particular job is dangerously stressed, either by its particular specification of duties and demands, or by the wider social changes to which a particular occupation may be vulnerable. But when people in *any* job become anxious, depressed or physically ill as a result of doing that job we can in fact begin to identify a fairly limited number of common stressing forces which run through all jobs, but which have a more potent and possibly dangerous influence at specific times and for specific people.

In this book, we have organised these themes under four headings:

Personality. Each individual brings to his or her job their own personal temperament, their early experiences, their own likes and dislikes, abilities and weaknesses, and their own methods of trying to do the job and surviving in the workplace. There are particular forms of personality which, coupled with certain jobs, can predispose people to feel either acutely stressed or deeply satisfied by what they do.

Control and load. Each job varies in how many and what kind of demands it makes on workers. Jobs also vary tremendously in how much responsibility and participation in decision-making they give to individuals. The interaction between the latitude a worker has to make decisions and the load he has to carry is a major factor in determining how stressful a job is. Other related factors include how much variety there is in the job, how much chance it gives you to exercise and develop skills, whether it involves deadlines, how clear it is what you are trying to achieve, and knowing whether you've achieved it or not.

Other people. Every job varies in how much you have to work with and get on with other people – superiors, colleagues and subordinates. Other people at work can be a major source of job stress. So can the clients or members of the public you have to deal with, and it very much matters what you have to *do* for these people – from connecting them to a phone call to counselling them on their life problems.

Change. Finally, change of any kind can be a source of stimulation or a constant and demanding worry. This includes personal changes at work from promotion and re-training (or the lack of it), problems of job-security and job-loss through to changes in society involving people's images of themselves and the value of what they do. For example, many more women are now employed both in executive jobs and part-time, unskilled jobs than was the case a few years ago. At the same time many men face the prospect of seeing the job they have spent their lives doing change dramatically or even disappear.

In the rest of this book, we'll look in much more detail at the way these four groups of factors can make or mar a job. We'll also suggest some proven and practical ways in which you can go about identifying what influence they have in your work life and what can be done to make them work for you, and not against you.

CHAPTER THREE

Personality and stress

It's a commonsense observation that what stresses one person might not stress another, and that some people seem more vulnerable to stress generally while others are extremely resistant to a wide variety of stressing situations. We all have different personalities, different strengths and weaknesses, and different interests or aversions. But is there any way of making sense of these differences and relating them to the stresses that people encounter at work? There have been many attempts to classify personality and understand the reasons why people are so different from one another. A lot of people firmly believe in the ancient notion that their personalities are shaped by the particular stars they were born under or that people can be classified according to the style of their handwriting, but alas there is no scientific evidence to support these beliefs, despite some recent interesting attempts to assess their validity.

However, we still carry with us many medieval or even older ideas. For example, we still use terms based on the descriptions of types first devised by Hippocrates a couple of thousand years ago. Hippocrates believed that people's personalities depended on whether they had an excess of one of four vital fluids in their bodies. He thus made a four-way classification of people as either Choleric, which meant they were weak and irritable and liable to stomach upsets; Melancholic – introspective – emotional and worrying; Sanguine – hard-working and durable; or Phlegmatic – slow and calm (but with a tendency to plumpness, he noticed).

Much later on in the late nineteenth century the psychologist Ivan Pavlov, who gave us the word 'conditioning', developed his own system of classifying people's personalities. Pavlov's classifications originally arose from his preoccupation with conditioning responses in dogs and his observations of how different dogs responded to the stresses and strains of taking part in his conditioning experiments. Pavlov eventually classified people as either the excitory type, who were rapidly disabled by excitement under stress; the inhibitory type, who he noticed were paralysed by stress; the lively type, normally excited but controlled under stress; and the calm type, who reacted with equanimity and passivity under stress.

What's interesting about both of these men's observations, although they lived so far apart in time, is that they both make fairly commonsense distinctions between excitable and calm people and between lively, outgoing and quieter, inward-looking people. Both of them believed that these traits were mostly inherited, but they thought they could be influenced to some extent by subsequent experience. The early experiments of Pavlov and his American counterpart George Watson eventually provided the basis for a whole approach to the study of behaviour within psychology known as 'behaviourism'. Behaviourism was based on the idea that all our behaviour is strongly directed by the environment around us and the kind of conditioned responses that we make to that environment, whether we like it or not.

Inheritors of the behaviourist tradition, notably in this country Professor Jeffrey Gray and his colleagues at the Maudsley Hospital in London, believe that we also inherit certain key dispositions which influence what kind of environment we feel happiest in, the way we learn to cope with events and the amount of stress we can cope with. He puts it like this:

There are certain very broad ways in which people differ from each other, and they have pervasive effects on virtually every aspect of behaviour. And if you look at those kinds of differences in personality, we believe that about half of the differences between people's personality can be accounted for by the genes they inherit from their parents.

Three of the more important ways in which people differ from each other we call sensation-seeking, extraversion and neuroticism. *Sensation-seeking* is rather what it sounds like. There are some people who just love to do things for a dare. They'll learn to go scuba-diving, or parachute-jumping or hang-gliding, while other people wouldn't dream of doing anything quite like that. *Extroversion* is also concerned with that kind of seeking-out of experience, but it's more to do with the seeking-out of social experience. An extrovert is someone who greatly enjoys being with other people, he's very gregarious, while the opposite is an individual we call an introvert, who prefers to be on his own, likes reading books, more solitary pursuits and so on. Then there is the dimension of personality known as *neuroticism* [which describes those] who generally show great emotional responses to most events. People who are less neurotic are much more calm and phlegmatic.

The important thing to remember is that all these kinds of differences between people are related to very basic aspects of the physiology of the body and the physiology of the brain. They depend a great deal on inherited characteristics and they affect virtually everything that people do and their feelings about it, including their jobs.

The simplest way one can measure these personality characteristics is just by asking people to fill in a questionnaire which consists of a series of very basic questions about everyday life. And then we score the questionnaire, add up the Yeses and Nos, and get values for people on these dimensions of extroversion, neuroticism, sensation-seeking and so on.

Because these aspects of personality reflect something quite basic about what's going on in the nervous system, we can also measure people's personality by looking at their behaviour, or even taking measurements of their physiology. For example, some people are much more emotional than others, and these are the ones who score high on the so-called neuroticism scale. Someone who is highly emotional will respond dramatically to a very simple stimulus, a loud noise for example, that won't affect somebody who's much less emotional.

Another way to measure personality goes much deeper still, Professor Gray believes; it is possible to measure the rate at which people form conditioned responses.

If you blow a puff of air into someone's eye, he will of course automatically shut his eye-lid. If you regularly precede that puff of air with a small tone, then he will eventually automatically shut his eye-lid on hearing the tone, before the air puff is ever delivered. We know that people who score high on the introversion scale of the questionnaire learn this conditioned reflex, as it's called, much more quickly than people who get extrovert scores.

What's important is that the simple physiological reflex, the rate at which an individual learns to close his eye-lid, actually predicts his answers on a very complex questionnaire that asks questions about everyday human life, and that questionnaire in turn predicts something about how the individual might break down under stress. So the chain is complete from simply physiology to complex behaviour – even to breakdown.

All these effects have implications for the kind of job that suits different kinds of people, and minimises the likelihood of stress.

Everybody works best if they're in circumstances that they like and, as you would expect, introverts prefer to work more on their own, while extroverts prefer to work in company. People who are highly emotional tend to react much more adversely to conditions of extreme demand than people who take stress more calmly. People who like strong sensations in life can happily undertake very risky jobs which the rest of us might refuse to do. So it's clearly important to fit the right people to the right job.

So Professor Gray and his colleagues make the astonishing claim that our most personal and unique interests and preferences have a direct and fairly simple relation to the kind of nervous system we inherit, and that this will predict what kind of job we will be happiest in, and what will stress us most about that job. They believe that the most powerful predictions about our hopes and fears can be made according to where we come in the sensation-seeking, introvert – extrovert scale and the stability –

neuroticism scale as measured by their tests devised at the Institute of Psychiatry at the Maudsley Hospital.

There are two very clear implications from their work. One is that some people are more vulnerable to stress than others, and the other is that we are all more vulnerable to stress if put in the wrong job.

Square pegs in round holes

The stress of being in the wrong job can drive a person from it even when they are well qualified, well paid and considered to be doing well by their employers. We spoke to a young Scot who graduated from Glasgow University in 1979 and quickly got a responsible job with an insurance company which he now plans to leave.

> It's basically an office job, a desk job dealing largely with paperwork, and dealing with various types of insurance claims. The only connection with people outside the office is on the telephone. A fair percentage of the work involves figures and involves a calculation of, say, wage losses, calculations of damages etc., and these calculations can be quite intricate and quite involved. I just don't think I'm the type of person who can find any interest or satisfaction in doing that kind of work – I don't really have the aptitude for working with figures.
>
> In this day and age it's almost frivolous I think to talk about job satisfaction, but I think one of the problems that I have with the job is that I don't get any satisfaction from it at all. The main problem is really boredom. Added to that is the fact that I generally don't think I'm really good at what I'm doing and I'm surrounded by people who are good at what they are doing. I find it frustrating, I find it really depressing. I just don't want to continue spending my time doing that kind of work – the benefits if any that I get from it, are more than outweighed by the disadvantages to me.

Dr John Nicholson, who is both a lecturer in psychology

and an industrial consultant told us why he believes that experiences like these are much more common than most of us realise.

It's ironic because people blame unemployment for causing stress, and they also blame employment for causing stress. The real reason why working can be quite literally bad for many of us is that we are not fitted to the job that we are doing. It's a square peg in a round hole and nothing is actually more stressful than that. We know that people who are dissatisfied with their jobs and malsuited to them eventually show physical and psychological symptoms of their stress. Certainly, one of the most important aspects of fitting personalities to jobs is really one's orientation towards people, and this is very closely bound up with the psychological notion of introversion and extroversion.

Some people seem to be almost hungry for others and need a lot of personal contact, a lot of people around them, and that can have all sorts of consequences for the type of workplace that suits them, as well as the sort of work that they do. If you a 'person-orientated' person then it makes sense to go for professions ranging from doctor to receptionist – all the jobs that require constant contact with people. If on the other hand you are happy with ideas and you are happy with your own company, happy with things rather than people, then perhaps you should be working with concepts or with machinery.

Dr Nicholson believes that careful personnel selection is a vital and largely unrecognised means of reducing job stress.

It's probably never been more important than it is today to get the right person doing the right job. We live in a time of extremely high unemployment. You have a job you advertise, where once you'd get fifteen applications you now get perhaps fifteen hundred applications, and that makes the task of selection that much more difficult. Also, thanks to legislation, it is extremely difficult if you're an employer to lose people who, for whatever reason, were placed in the wrong jobs. For both these reasons, personnel selection is probably more important to them than it's ever been. That means that the search for a reliable means of fitting the right person to the job is on, and a wide variety of procedures are available.

It's really a question of just using everything that's to hand, and that will include some personality testing. You have to decide what aspects of personality are important and that won't be the same for all sorts of jobs. It may involve attitudes towards people, it may involve ability to handle stress, it may involve an ability to work with members of the opposite sex, to be flexible. It may involve an ability to suppress personal ambition. These are all different aspects of personality that might well come into the job. . . .

Then you must think about the job itself and really analyse it, to see what demands it makes on people, make a list of them, and again see how well the person in front of you suits those demands. . . . In today's climate many people will tend to believe that any job is better than no job. I don't accept that, and as a psychologist it seems to me absolutely clear that doing the wrong job, if you're sufficiently ill-fitted to it, may be ultimately much more damaging to you than doing no job at all.

More and more firms are beginning to use consultancy services to advise them on job selection and promotion, particularly of important personnel, but as the number of working days lost due to stress in Britain rises steadily (we believe that at least 40 million working days are lost now each year), a few consultancy firms have come into existence which combine both personnel selection techniques and health screening in an attempt to spot individuals vulnerable to stress in their work at an early stage.

One company was recently set up by the occupational psychologist Dr Christopher Ridgeway and a group of physicians and clinical psychologists. This company is called Executive Health Screening. They have developed a procedure which involves a preliminary interview with a doctor followed by routine physical health checks, and then each client runs through a battery of personality tests of various kinds. One group of tests measures the kind of personality characteristics which are often used as a basis for job selection. They measure factors like intelligence, maturity, adaptability, capacity for leadership, neuroticism and so on. Other tests are designed to spot factors like anxiety, depression and a sense of alienation. The tests are administered via 600 questions presented on a personal computer and 'marked' by the computer itself, producing an instant readout which compares the profile of test results against the 'normal' personality.

Dr Ridgeway stresses that the computer-generated profile is used as a preliminary filter only. After analysing it, he and his colleagues give further interviews to clients whose test results indicate that they may be under stress, so that they can finally decide what particular strategy they can best offer them. This could consist of in-house counselling, referral to other agencies or advice on how they might alter the pattern of their working lives. Dr Ridgeway stresses that he is not acting as a 'weak-link' detector for firms who wish to get rid of people who can't cope. Instead he is attempting to help both the firm and the individual by either helping clients to see how to do their own job properly again, or advising them on what might be a better position or even a better job for them.

Dr Ridgeway recognises that some people are more vulnerable to stress than others, but he doesn't believe that this is a major factor in the more common forms of job stress.

> There are some people who are particularly neurotic who will have been that way for some period of time. What's far more normal is that it's somebody who's had a perfectly normal and acceptable career, and because of the changing nature of our society is placed in a position where they can no longer cope. They're given responsibility very early in their lives and that is sustained for a long period, which is obviously quite difficult for them to manage. They're required to learn new skills, faster than they've ever been required before. Their decisions are checked more than they've ever been before. These kind of factors are likely to

cause even the most resilient of people to have some degree of stress, but obviously people vary greatly in terms of the ability they've got to cope with the stresses placed upon them.

John Nicholson agrees that our vulnerability to stress very much depends not only on our general anxiety and neuroticism levels but on the extent to which we are asked to meet demands for which we are not temperamentally suited.

What makes us the people that we are is a mixture of biology and experience. We certainly inherit a sort of nervous system and brain that predisposes us to develop certain attitudes towards the world and other people. On the one hand you might be born with a brain that is not programmed to seek out other people and get on well with them, but on the other hand if very early in life that same person has had some very fortunate relationships and there were people around to encourage them to spend time with others they might well develop in almost a different direction. In fact, most of us simply proceed in the direction that is started by our inherited biological factors and this can make it very difficult to change. There are, for example, many businessmen who rise to the top of their professions and suddenly find that they have to be not just good at their business but also good at handling other people, and these people often get into trouble when these new demands are made for which they are not suited.

Personality and early experience

Good job-fit is almost certainly the most important single factor to affect personal job satisfaction or stress, but although it's useful to talk in general terms of the stresses due to a misfit between our temperaments and the job situation we find ourselves in, it would be even more valuable to know exactly what kind of events upset particular kinds of people, and what shaped the way they react to stress. Some interesting and valuable work on this has been done recently by Dr Jenny Firth, working at the Social and Applied Psychology Unit in Sheffield.

Over a four-year period Dr Firth investigated the stresses experienced by a group of about forty managerial and professional workers in a variety of occupations, referred to her by doctors as suffering from stress. She was primarily trying to find out the value of therapies based on prescriptions for behaviour (like relaxation and anxiety, management training, assertiveness and social skills training, and time management and delegation techniques) and to compare them with more traditional psychotherapy based on individual discussions between a therapist and client. This aims to explore which aspects of a person's early experience might unconsciously predispose them to stress.

> This is part of psychodynamic therapy which goes right back to Freud and has been carried on for years. It doesn't usually emphasise the work situation as much as we've been doing, because our particular clinic concentrates on work problems, but the general idea is the same. The idea is that your early relationships all have their difficulties, creating fears and expectations of behaviour in other people, and these relationships at times of difficulty in present life can be re-enacted in some way. So in difficult situations bells will ring and you'll start behaving in a way that perhaps you behaved when you were a child, or you expected other people to behave to you when you were a child. It's very hard sometimes for people to see that things have actually changed and so they go on the same way, year after year. Both in marriage and work.

Dr Firth first noticed that many of the people she talked to weren't even aware of how stressed they were until help was offered, but just discovering the extent of their problem often went a long way to relieving their symptoms. As she interviewed one person after another, discussing not only their present work problems but the problems and worries of their early childhood, Dr Firth began to see at least three consistent themes emerging.

First of all she identified a group of people who tended to feel overworked, worried and uncertain and to have very high expectations of themselves. They were often not able to delegate to anyone else. We encountered a typical story of this kind in our own researches. This is the experience of a trade union official who was sent to a new part of the country to organise the local union structure. He was able to set his own objectives, but every time he did so he felt compelled to enlarge them.

> Well, I got into it – deeper and deeper and deeper – and I really couldn't see the end. I was getting more and more involved and working harder and harder, longer hours. Every time I got something going it created more work. The worst thing of all was the feeling of not being able to cope. Everyday, I'd go in to the office and the pile would be higher. . . . I couldn't bear to go and face things every morning. I was feeling miserable, I was snapping with the children, I was nasty to my wife. And that's not me. I'm normally a happy, carefree sort of person.

Eventually, he broke down completely.

> First of all they just put me on tranquillisers, and I had some interviews with a psychiatrist, and that was it. After three months I went back to work. And people were very supportive for a while, but people can't carry you, and I felt too that I was a passenger when I'm not, I'm an achiever. I am good at my job, and I know I'm good at my job. And when the pressure came on again I felt the same symptoms coming back. I felt once I was drowning in the work.

According to Dr Firth this kind of person often has a background where as a child they thought they were loved mainly for their ability to achieve. These patients often tried to please her during therapy, just as they have always tried to please their parents. It's a consistent theme in the kind of therapy which Dr Firth offers that the behaviour of the client with the therapist often resembles the behaviour they first developed in their childhood. The trade union official said:

> I'm a terrible person, I'm a perfectionist. I'm very, very highly motivated. I try and do everything better than it

needs to be done. I think I get some of my behaviour difficulties from my father. He's a missionary. And he went
out to save the world, literally. And I've tried to be too
perfectionist about everything I've wanted to do. If I've
written a set of minutes I always want to put Letraset on
the top. I want to have a nice layout. I want to do it in
two colours. Whereas what I should really be doing is
thinking about getting the minutes out of the way and
getting where I want to go, rather than worry about the
way I'm getting there.

Eventually this particular man was recommended to a behavioural psychologist who pointed out to him his perfectionist
and over-ambitious strategies. She told him how to set himself a
reasonable limit and some basic principles of time managing,
and so far this seems to work well for him.

Another typical group of patients were those who on promotion to a position that they wanted, and which they were perfectly capable of doing, felt themselves overwhelmed, depressed
and unable to act. We spoke to a talented young woman who
became director of a well-known provincial theatre. This was
the peak of her career so far. For the first few months she coped
with the problems of her new post well, and then . . .

I'd got to the point of success, when I was settled, when the
theatre was on target, when we'd had a series of successful
productions, the financial problems were beginning to be
sorted out, I had actually turned the place round, everything
was hunky-dory. At that point I got the director's equivalent
of writer's block. I just didn't have an idea in my head. And
of course actually what I'm paid for is to have ideas, because
like any artist if you can't create something from nothing,
then you're not an artist any more, so I froze really. Any
artist who experiences not being able to function, any
person who experiences not being able to do their job is
obviously going to suffer severe depression and I did. I was
extremely depressed. I found life virtually impossible to toler-
ate – that's why I went for help.

She went for help to Dr Firth who discovered that her early

background was very similar to that of many other people suffering from the same kind of problem. Like many of them, she revealed feelings of unresolved grief for the parent of her own sex, coupled with an early sense of responsibility for her parents' feelings.

> What I observed as a child was that my father was very powerful and that my mother, even though she worked and was a very established woman in her own right, seemed to be experiencing high stress all the time. I think I made some kind of almost unconscious choice early on that I was going to be my father, not my mother in terms of my career. But of course, sexually, I wanted to be my mother as well, and so the more successful I got ... the more I found myself thrown between those two pictures of the way life can be lived out.

After a series of the eight one-hour discussion sessions which Dr Firth gives to each client, the director now feels that she knows herself much better.

> Well, it's a while back now and I guess I'm sort of used to my new self now, but I now enjoy life, I now enjoy the conflicts, whereas before I felt that any conflict I came into meant that I'd failed.

The third group that Dr Firth observed were people chronically unable to get on with other people at work – often aggressive, hostile and competitive. Many of the people we spoke to, to investigate what have been called the 'type A' characteristics, associated with heart disease, spoke to us of their work and colleagues this way. Excerpts of those interviews are quoted in the next chapter. Dr Firth believes that many hostile people come from family backgrounds characterised by a lack of trust, a concern not to get too close in case they were deceived or humiliated, and a history of much rivalry with their peers or brothers or sisters.

Although the original research was intended to examine the effectiveness of techniques for changing people's behaviour, many of which we will look at later in this book, Dr Firth found that just revealing and talking about these very early problems did a great deal to relieve her clients' feelings of stress, and helped them modify their behaviour at work. She is now convinced that there is a consistent relationship between certain kinds of stress symptoms which many display at work and their early experience.

> I know that a lot of people would be sceptical to think it's something to do with early environment that later on makes them act in a certain way at work, getting into fights with colleagues and things like this. But all I can say is that after a while the pattern is there. When clients do come to you, you can make predictions about what their early environment was, because of the patterns they're presenting at work.
>
> But I don't think you're stuck with that early experience. I think that for most of us it works very well and in the areas where it *doesn't* work very well, you're not stuck with it. You can change it, understand it and then learn how to do something about it.

But perhaps the last word might go to the theatre director:

> I think I had the problem of a lot of the middle-class intelligentsia, that read paperback Freud, and think, Well, I know all about that. But until you've actually lived through what those conflicts are – in my case until I'd lived through those conflicts in therapy when I realised what I was doing, playing out old conflicts with my parents in terms of my job or whatever, or in terms of my son – they couldn't get released. They were unfinished business, I guess.

Presenting Problems and Themes for Therapy

Presenting Problems	*Themes for therapy*
High investment in work alone	
Overwork	Only loved for achievements
High expectations	Still trying to please 'parent':
Worry	boss/therapist
Uncertainty	
Inability to delegate	
Poor relationship with colleagues	Lack of trust: fear of getting close and being
Can't get on with colleagues	tricked/humiliated
Can't work in group	
Poor relationship with subordinates	Competition: rivalry with siblings/therapist
Promotion problems	
Too much responsibility	Meaning of responsibility:
Depression on promotion	responsible for parents'/
Avoidance of promotion	workers'/therapists' happiness
	Loss of same-sex parent
Role conflicts	
Conflicts about success	Exploration of the meaning of
Conflicts about career	the conflict in terms of early relationships

(From Dr Jenny Firth, *Journal of Occupational Psychology*, 1985, Vol. 58, p. 139)

CHAPTER FOUR

Personality and your job

Individual responses to work

It's clear that there are influences from both inherited character-istics and very early family experiences which help to determine what is the right occupation or position for a particular person. People are also influenced in the approach they bring to any job and the satisfaction or stress they get from it, by the overall picture they have developed – as they grow up – of who they are, how the world works and how to get on and prosper in it. They are not always correct, however. A number of psychologists have tried to determine if there are typical ways of coping with problems and tasks which might predispose particular workers to stress. Four types of approach to the workplace emerge frequently in the literature as making people particularly vulner-able to work stress.

Type 1. Unassertive approach – potential relationships problems. People who can't easily say No can easily slip into situations where they are stressed by demands made on them – in tasks they have too easily agreed to do. They may be made anxious, exhausted or even phobic by over-demand and, because of their reluctance to express their resentment, they may also suffer from depression and inner conflict. They can sometimes also suffer from boredom, having entered jobs which they know won't really challenge them. They may be over-sensitive, lacking in confi-dence and unable to carry a task through unless pushed.

Type 2. Obsessional approach – potential control problems. Some people can cope happily with demanding jobs providing the tasks involved are predictable and stable. They tend to be particularly fond of all the little traditions, details and rituals of the job. They are often extremely conscientious, competent and hard-working. However, if the job changes suddenly (they are promoted, for example) or the work load increases beyond a certain level or there is too much extraneous disturbance or change in the job situation, they may not only become even less flexible, but may develop various typical stress-related physical illnesses.

Type 3. Stimulus-seeker – potential problems of stability. By contrast a group of people has been identified who seem to feel secure only when things are changing. Pathologically stimulus-seeking, they typically seek out a succession of demanding and exciting occupations – often involving physical or financial risk. Alternatively, they may try to organise a conventional job so that it involves cutting corners, taking chances and winning temporary triumphs. The chief danger for this sort of person is that they may become addicted to stress-induced adrenalin and noradrenalin; they may also get themselves into inextricable situations. They more commonly show stress behaviours like heavy smoking and alcohol drinking than mental or physical illness symptoms.

Type 4. Ambitious (sometimes called Type A) – potential problems of control. People who are compulsively busy, aggressive and impatient encounter a number of job-related stresses mostly initiated by themselves. These are reflected in a wide range of minor illnesses from which they tend to suffer, like migraine and ulcers. Most significantly, however, they are also particularly prone to high blood pressure and heart disease. The frequency and severity of this stress response and the widespread incidence of this kind of behaviour, particularly among influential managerial and supervisory staff, has meant that it has received a great deal of research attention. We will discuss this particular type in more detail a little later on.

When they generate problems, these types of personal approach to work can be treated from two directions. On the one hand, individuals can be given some counselling and insight into the ineffectiveness of some of their work strategies. Obsessional workers can be encouraged to attend stress management groups, and the unassertive may attend the assertiveness classes and social skills groups which we discuss in more detail in later chapters. The over-ambitious and compulsive stimulus-seekers are harder to deal with, but as we will see, efforts are now being made to develop procedures for helping them to gain insight into the ultimate unproductiveness of their behaviour.

Alternatively, these people's problems can also be seen as problems of *management*. If people cannot recognise their own particular weaknesses and vulnerabilities, it falls even more acutely to senior supervisors and personnel staff to make sure that they are protected and not put into positions they can't cope with, or promoted to positions for which they are not temperamentally suited. Many workplaces are still conceived of as *hierarchies* with a chain from lower to higher positions, when we might much more usefully and realistically understand them as consisting of groups of people working side by side and carrying out the particular functions for which they are particularly suited.

Check your personality type

To complete this quiz, just tick the questions to which you answer Yes.

1 I find it difficult to say 'no' to any kind of demand on me.
2 I get restless if I am not involved in several different activities.
3 I would describe myself as a dedicated type of person.
4 'A place for everything and everything in its place' is my motto.
5 Disagreements with people really upset me a lot.
6 I like to make a thoroughly good job of all that I do.
7 I get bored very easily.
8 I like to see things through whatever the obstacles.
9 I believe you can only get ahead by taking risks.
10 I find it very hard to take or give criticism.
11 My personal standards are high and demanding.

12 I go for long periods thinking only of one ambition.

13 I think everyone is given just one real chance somewhere in life.

14 I dislike having my daily routine interrupted.

15 I have great difficulty in leaving situations when I have had enough.

16 Months can often go by before I realise I have not seen my friends.

17 I usually put myself second in family matters.

18 I believe it is essential to speculate in order to accumulate.

19 Imperfections of any sort upset me considerably.

20 Work is its own reward.

21 I am impulsive in my relationships.

22 I would rather have one too many appointments in my diary than one too few.

23 I find it difficult to express my needs to others.

24 I am often preoccupied when those close to me are having fun.

25 My motto is 'Faint heart never won fair lady'.

26 The people I work with know that when I say a thing I mean it.

27 I have very little or no privacy in my life.

28 I dislike having loose ends at work or at home.

29 Sex plays a very secondary part in my life.

30 I become very agitated if people fail to carry out simple instructions.

31 I always seem to lose arguments.

32 I often have difficulty finishing off what I have started.

33 I think the best part of an affair is the thrill of the chase.

34 Being bound up in the day's events often spoils sex for me.

35 I find it difficult to introduce myself and make relationships.

36 I sometimes wonder if I have missed out on relationships by working so hard on my career.

37 I do not find it easy to express my emotions.

38 I tend to worry just as much whether the problem is a large one or a small one.

39 As soon as I have reached one career goal, I set up a higher one.

40 I have sometimes spoiled relationships by having too much going on at once.

TO SCORE

TYPE 1: Score one point if you have answered 'YES' to the following questions:
1, 5, 10, 15, 17, 23, 27, 31, 35, 37.

TYPE 2: Score one point if you have answered 'YES' to the following questions:
4, 6, 11, 14, 19, 24, 28, 34, 38.

TYPE 3: Score one point if you have answered 'YES' to the following questions:
3, 8, 12, 16, 20, 22, 26, 29, 36, 39.

TYPE 4: Score one point if you have answered 'YES' to the following questions:
2, 7, 9, 13, 18, 21, 25, 32, 33, 40.

You now have 4 totals – one for each 'type' described on pages 52–3.

A score of 5 or more in any one section would indicate that you fit into the personality type for which that score was obtained.

A score of 8, 9, or 10 in any one section would indicate that you may now, or in the future, experience some of the stresses listed for that type.

High scores in *more than one* section would indicate a high risk of stress responses.

(Originally prepared by Dr Robert Sharpe and Alice Harper)

Type A and how to beat it

Certain high-status managerial and sales jobs bring with them a good deal of autonomy and flexibility, and at the same time a good deal of responsibility. Since people in these types of job are left largely to their own devices without direct day-to-day supervision, they need to have a high level of self-motivation in order to produce results – and indeed to survive. Another essential quality is the ability to keep their ultimate aims in mind and determine the best method of achieving them. This will involve assessing the relative importance of different aspects of the job, determining priorities and allocating the *right* amount of time and effort to spend on each particular task. All these are considerable and complex requirements.

This type of job is likely to attract a particular type of personality – people who are competitive, hard-driving, ambitious and time-conscious. Moreover, the job is likely further to develop these characteristics in the person doing it.

A company salesman, whose brief is simply to meet his budget, illustrates this type of job well. David, a salesman working for a chemicals company, has complete independence to decide how to go about achieving his necessary sales figures. He is very conscious of the importance of personal relationships with each one of his customers and puts a lot of effort into establishing and maintaining these. In order to visit all his customers in person, he finds himself having to travel thousands of miles each year. The amount of driving he has to do can be a source of stress to him, and the unpredictable timing of long journeys makes it difficult for him to schedule his time. He is constantly aware of the importance of punctuality and reliability in keeping the confidence of his customers.

> You're responsible for selling your company's products. In my case, I make my own appointments, I approve the budget that is allocated to me. It is then your responsibility to meet that budget and the only way you can do that is to get out, meet the customers and sell to them. You're looking for repetitive business and to do that you must really get around, motivate yourself, irrespective of what the weather is like, whether you don't particularly feel like it that day or not. Things don't just happen, you've got to make them happen. You have got to get to know customers, customers have to get to know and accept you and like you and trust you, because you are really after business which you are hoping to get year in, year out, and it takes a lot of effort.
>
> I would think probably in this job, self-motivation is all important. If it doesn't come naturally to you, I don't see any way you can make a success of this type of selling, or

any type of selling. You must get yourself out, you must get yourself to the customers, you must do the thousand and one things the customers require, whether that means staying late, going out for a meal at night or whatever.

Any selling job is a twenty-four hour job. There's no way this will ever be a nine-to-five job. Subconsciously one is trying the whole time. You never really switch off even at night time, or even when you're playing golf at the weekends. It's amazing.

David is successful in his job because he is highly motivated to win new customers and gets great satisfaction when he does. Although he shows no sign of suffering from stress, he does find it difficult to switch off and relax when he is away from work. This necessarily high degree of involvement and commitment can, however, cause problems for a certain kind of person. People without the necessary self-motivation will fail in this type of job, but at the other end of the scale, people can be highly self-motivated but unable to direct their energies effectively, and (something that often goes hand in hand with this) never know when to stop. These people have been called Type As.

'Type A' behaviour is a term first coined thirty years ago by two heart specialists in California – Meyer Friedman and Ray Rosenman. They were intrigued to find that only the fronts of the chairs in their waiting-room needed to be re-covered. They attributed this to the rushed, impatient characters of their cardiac patients, who were so anxious to get in and out as quickly as possible that they were unable to sit back and relax. Friedman and Rosenman conducted an eight-year study of over 1500 men to investigate what they called the Type A behaviour pattern. They defined Type A men as those who were highly competitive and ambitious, spoke rapidly and interrupted others frequently and were unusually often seized by hostility and anger. They found that these men had roughly twice as many heart attacks as the 'Type B' men who did not have Type A characteristics and took life more calmly.

Research has continued, principally in America, into Type A behaviour and its relation to heart disease. It emerges that although Type A behaviour appears to many people to be a good route to the top, it can actually be extremely dangerous, as Len, a former company director found out.

I think you could say that perhaps in retrospect my problems started in, say, 1970. I joined an American company, I was quickly made general manager. At the time I was living in Northampton and working in Farnham in Surrey. I was travelling there, on a Monday, working during the week. I could be anywhere during the week, going back home on Friday, and that I think is where the stress part started.

I would think I was putting in something like twelve hours a day, and it was a very long and pressurised day. And of course you're living in a hotel, which is a lonely sort of existence, from Monday to Friday. It's all part of what has to be done to run a successful company. I was attempting to make the company that I had been made general manager of successful; and this was really it, if that was successful, I was successful. I was really going at eleven-tenths. It culminated then in a serious illness, and I was told by a specialist that this was caused by the pace that I had been going at. I had pleurisy. I had awful pains in my back and I went home and my wife called a doctor. The following Thursday I was in hospital with blood clots. I was due to come out and I had another massive pulmonary embolism which goes into the lungs. My wife was called late at night. It was a traumatic period. This specialist reiterated, 'You must slow it down' and I didn't take any notice of him. I just ignored it, because I still hadn't achieved what I'd set out to achieve. It's all very well a specialist saying 'slow down'. How do you slow down? You've still got a company to run, you're still in charge, you've got a family to support, and I totally ignored it and just carried on.

[Eventually] it was decided that in order to give me a rejuvenated sort of existence, I should have open heart surgery. The specialist whom I was under said that if you don't get off the loud pedal then you can have this type of operation every five years, and you really must rethink what you're doing. Well, I did rethink what I was doing, because

I really had to take his advice. I've made a conscious decision, I've got off the loud pedal.

I would not want to be classed as a failure within the confines of the business that I was in. My company had a good name. I think my colleagues and I had a good name. But I felt in my own mind that I failed because I didn't achieve what I set out to achieve. . . . Maybe now I feel that I have failed because I have got fifteen years still to go of a career that perhaps now I can't finish. So by doing what I did, perhaps I failed.

Origins of Type A behaviour. Various theories exist as to why people develop a Type A behaviour pattern. In many industries, people in the 'go-go' jobs are encouraged by senior management to push themselves as hard as they can. Young trainees and representatives who first enter middle management are particularly vulnerable to this kind of pressure. It's obviously possible to develop Type A behaviour characteristics simply as an attempt to survive in an over-demanding organisation, and this has been shown to happen often.

Arousal level check list

Are you working in a Type A environment? Look at the following list, and see which items you feel best describe what's expected of employees in your place of work.

1 In my job, they tell us you can only succeed by giving all your effort.
2 You don't usually get a lot of shocks and surprises – you usually know what's going to come up next.
3 You've got to think quickly, there and then, you can't make decisions tomorrow.
4 We process information every day, but never more than I can handle.
5 I often find it difficult to quieten down after work.
6 We don't often have to work to deadlines.
7 It's a job where you can never really relax.
8 In our job, you don't have to complete tasks as they come in.

9 If we don't come up with the goods or make the right decision, it could be disastrous.

10 In our job we spend a fair amount of time just planning –
to make sure we're well ahead of any problems.

For the odd-numbered questions, score 2 for every Yes answer,
and for even-numbered questions, score 2 for each No. The
higher your score, the more arousal your job demands of you.
If you have a score of 16 or more, your job is asking too much
of you, and you need to take steps to reduce the burden it puts
on you. A score in the 12–16 range indicates a fairly high
arousal level at work – be careful not to become swamped. A
score of 6–12 suggests that your job is relatively peaceful.
Below 6, and you have a very laid-back job. Are you sure you
aren't bored?

Alternatively, Type A behaviour may be one form of escape
from depression. If a Type A can direct all his energies and
concentration into keeping permanently busy and always on the
move, he will never have time to sit still and confront things he
would prefer not to. Other theories have suggested that the roots
of Type A behaviour lie in deep hostility or cynicism and that
this is what drives the Type A relentlessly on. Certainly Type As
typically express feelings of anger and resentment against other
people whom they perceive as inefficient, stupid or lazy, and it
appears that feelings like these are one of the most characteristic
symptoms of Type As. This can help when attempts are being
made actually to identify a real Type A.

Identifying Type As. We probably all know people who seem to
fit the profile of the fully fledged Type A: impatient, ambitious,
competitive, hostile and obsessively trying to beat the clock.
Many people, however, will fall some way between Type A and
the more easy-going Type B, having some Type A characteristics
but perhaps not enough seriously to endanger their health. One
of the simplest ways to assess the extent of Type A behaviour in
an individual is by getting them to fill in a questionnaire, and
you can try the simplified version of this on page 62.

This method has its limitations, however, in that people don't always have very clear insights into their own behaviour. Dr Clive Wood, the author of *Living in Overdrive* and one of the people studying Type A behaviour in this country, has been looking at the value of American-style structured interviews to identify and assess Type A characteristics. While conducting a structured interview, Dr Wood notes not only the answers people give but also how they give them – how loudly and how fast they speak and whether they interrupt. He also monitors their heart rate and blood pressure. During the interview, as people re-live moments of anger and impatience which they have experienced, their heart rate and blood pressure often shoot up. This reflects the real-life situation in which the Type A allows himself to get upset or disturbed. His blood pressure may go up a dozen times or more a day and this is thought to contribute to bringing a heart attack closer.

Below is a short personality test extracted by Professor Cary Cooper from a longer questionnaire on behaviour and heart disease. For each of the eight questions below, choose one of the two phrases in capital letters which best applies to you.

Are you CASUAL ABOUT
   APPOINTMENTS   or NEVER LATE?
Are you NOT COMPETITIVE   or VERY COMPETITIVE?
Are you A GOOD LISTENER   or DO YOU OFTEN
                         INTERRUPT?
Are you NEVER RUSHED   or ALWAYS RUSHED?
Can you WAIT PATIENTLY   or are you IMPATIENT?
Do you usually EXPRESS   or do you tend to HIDE
   YOUR FEELINGS   YOUR FEELINGS?
Do you TAKE THINGS ONE or do you try to DO
   AT A TIME   LOTS OF THINGS AT ONCE?
Are you EASY-GOING   or are you HARD DRIVING?

If most of the statements you have chosen are from the right-hand column you show characteristics of Type A behaviour. You are time-conscious, achievement-oriented and hard driving. You are also more likely to suffer a heart attack as a result and should think about slowing down. If most of the statements you have chosen are from the left-hand column then you are more of a Type B – less ambitious, more relaxed and likely to live longer.

How does Type A behaviour make you ill? Type A behaviour produces various physiological changes. It's associated with excessive activity of the endocrine system and the sympathetic nervous system. As the Type A typically oscillates into and out of high arousal, he also makes high demands on the para-sympathetic nervous system.

The Type A's characteristic excessive hormonal response to stress has been illustrated in experiments. It was found that young Type A men doing mental arithmetic showed a more marked stress response, in terms of increased blood flow to the muscles and raised secretion of adrenalin and cortisol, than did Type B men doing the same task. When they were performing a 'vigilance task' (watching a video and pressing a button when a particular display of letters came up) Type A men showed an abnormal increase in blood levels of testosterone.

Along with the well-established degenerative effects on the heart and circulation of high adrenalin and high cortico-steroid blood levels produced by the arousing sympathetic nervous system (which we discussed in Chapter One), it now appears that continuous over-exposure to noradrenalin, produced as part of the parasympathetic system's efforts to calm Type As down again, also has dangerous effects. Dr Terry Looker has identified at least three ways in which a heart attack can be caused by the over-production of the hormone noradrenalin.

1 Noradrenalin constricts blood vessels. In someone suffering from coronary artery disease, the arteries become partially blocked by the growth of tissue and various deposits called plaque. When the blood vessels which supply blood to this plaque become constricted by over-production of nora-drenalin the plaque starts to decay, enabling blood to enter and form clots within it so that the arteries are still further obstructed.

2 Noradrenalin also has the effect of increasing the adhes-iveness of the blood cells used in clotting. This can cause

blood clots to form on the outside of plaque in the arteries, and again causes further obstruction.

3 Excessive noradrenalin can act directly on the heart muscles, causing change in the rhythm of the heart. At its most extreme, this can cause ventricular fibulation where the heart beats like a quivering jelly and effectively fails to pump blood. Unless this is immediately corrected, the person may die.

Clearly, it's extremely important that Type As somehow learn to stabilise their emotions and stop this destructive see-saw of hormone production.

What can be done to help Type As? In America, to a much greater extent than in this country, Type A behaviour is taken as a serious risk factor about which something can and should be done. Type As *can* be taught to modify their behaviour and, as they do so, their risk of having a heart attack does recede. Meyer Friedman successfully altered the Type A behaviour of over 500 American men who had already had one heart attack. The rate at which these men had a second heart attack was reduced to half the rate of a similar group who received conventional medical help but no advice on changing their behaviour.

The method which Meyer Friedman and his group used was to divide the Type As into small groups which met regularly over a period of three or four years. In these groups, the Type As were taught new living skills – for instance how to relax, how to talk more slowly, interrupt less and listen more, as well as how to organise and manage their work better. The groups would discuss situations which individual members had experienced, and work out how someone could have reacted without being rushed, impatient or angry, with a view to dealing better with a similar situation in the future.

British Type As may not be so amenable to this US-style 'talk in' and in any case it can be very difficult to persuade any Type A to change his behaviour on the grounds that it may do him serious damage in the future when, as yet, there are no perceptible signs that this is the case. Clive Wood is certain that Type A behaviour *can* be changed and thinks that the best way to get a Type A to change is to convince him that his behaviour is actually counter-productive.

> How do you tell a man of thirty in full flight that he's killing himself? I think the answer is quite simply that you don't. What you have to try to convince him is that he would actually get more done and he would feel better about what he's doing if he gave himself some time and space to plan and to act on his plans. So although the Type A pattern at first sight looks like the only possible formula for success, achievement, go-getting – actually when you get closer to it, it's really a recipe for disaster. What one has to try and do is to get it out of your life, and you'll find that when you do, not only do you have more chance of living longer but you're actually likely to be more productive at the same time. Type As don't perform any better, they just put more into it.

In this country, Dr Terry Looker is researching the usefulness of therapy groups like those used by Meyer Friedman for helping British Type As. It is too early for him yet to have seen clear results, but he is optimistic that this type of therapy will prove useful and even help to save lives in this country.

Some people have actually been able to alter their Type A behaviour for themselves, because they've been able to identify it in the first place, and thereafter have *wanted* to do something about it. Reg, now in his fifties, is a former top-line manager with a major international corporation. He's amazed now at the way he used to run his life.

> One of the things I always did was always do two jobs. So, when I was still in the Air Force I was selling insurance in the evenings and afternoons and all time off. When I worked as a shift foreman, I went to night classes. It wasn't technically a job, but it was more than just an eight-hour day.
>
> I've also always been very physically Type A, in the sense that I had to win that tennis match, played squash, played badminton – you name a sport and I played it. None of them terribly well, but all of them with great enthusiasm and high determination to win. . . . It was just a way of life,

didn't think about it even. Driving fast, playing sports, not sleeping a lot, really trying to pack twenty-five hours into every twenty-four-hour day and feeling slightly resentful about the amount of time that sleep took.

After years of this frenetic existence, Reg began to wake up to the fact that he wasn't doing himself much good.

I think the most significant point was where I'd invited an outside consultant to come and talk to managers about stress, and I suddenly heard the consultant describing me to an absolute tee. Part of that was a consciousness that . . . I was no longer as fit as I used to be and, talking to the consultant afterwards [I said] 'I've really taken to heart what you've been saying. I've decided that as of next week, I'm going to get up at five o'clock every morning, I'm going to go for a run, I'm going to do this, I'm going to do that.' And he just started to smile and we both finished up laughing because what I was doing was applying to my relaxation and leisure exactly the same characteristics as I'd been applying to work.

I suddenly had an image of an unbreakable toy . . . of me as an unbreakable toy that I was trying to destroy. That seemed a bit silly. Eventually I decided really to get more control over my own life. I thought, I can't change too much the way I am, but what I can do, if I take more control of my own life, is build in some checks and balances. So I quit my job – which was very well paid, had lots of perks – and went off working on my own.

I now work for myself, primarily as a consultant to other organisations. This enables me to say periodically, 'I'm going to have a four-day weekend or take the whole week off.' I have certain rules for myself like being home a certain amount, like meeting my little boy from school, or taking him to school. I just build in chores for myself like clearing a patch of the garden, sawing down that particular tree. I never drive more than fifty miles an hour in my home county, and I'm improving generally as less of a demon driver than I used to be.

I think the main overall feeling is that I've actually given myself far more things to worry about than when I worked for a large organisation, when I had a regular salary coming in, and I had all the car bills paid for me and all that sort of thing. But it matters much, much less mentally, emotionally, physically. I'm actually in better shape with all that extra worry than when I was leading what sounded like a nice calm secure life. But the main feeling I have is actually of greater control in all of this uncertainty.

I used to get indigestion, heartburn, never thought anything of it. I just thought it was a normal part of life. It was only after I stopped getting it, some months after changing my job and becoming more relaxed, that I suddenly woke up to the fact that I hadn't had it for months and began to put two and two together. I do have a worry about whether it's possible to still achieve things and be relaxed. You know, is there a pay-off if you don't put a lot of energy into something, if you don't really throw your heart and soul into something, can you still achieve as much as you have previously? And I think I do have points of frenzy. I do still cut down on sleep if I want to achieve something. So I haven't changed completely on that.

Even if you can't eradicate Type A tendencies in yourself, there's a good deal you can do to reduce them and keep them in check, provided you can identify them.

If you've failed the test on page 62 miserably, here are some positive steps, based on Professor Cary Cooper's advice, which you can take to avoid Type A behaviour. Have a good think about them. You may not be able to turn yourself into a Type B, but you can become an A-minus by recognising and altering your behaviour.

* Set goals and priorities. There isn't time to do everything. Do the essentials, delegate what you can and forgo the rest.
* Try not to make unnecessary appointments and unachievable deadlines. Protect your time by learning to say No and by leaving a fifteen-minute gap between appointments.
* Do only one thing at a time. Don't try to work and eat, for example.

* Take as many stress-free breaks as you can, even when working to a deadline.
* Spend some time alone each day doing nothing, even if only for a few minutes. Try to relax your body and mind entirely.
* Do not feel you always have to be right.
* Give more thought to the needs of others.
* Try to restrain yourself from constantly talking. Really listen to others and don't try to finish their sentences.
* Don't expect perfection in yourself or others. It will only make you frustrated and hostile.
* Use traffic jams and other potentially irritating situations to take some deep breaths and relax.
* Before rushing into a new task, ask yourself 'Will this be important five years from now? Must I do it now, or do I have time to think about the best way to accomplish it?'
* If you're a working wife, negotiate clearly with your husband on who does what at home.
* Relieve stress through exercise, relaxation, laughter, pleasurable activities. Make sure you have some fun in your life.

Have I got a stress prone personality?

This is a question that almost everyone who feels stressed has asked themselves at one time or another. There is a conventional wisdom that job stress simply seeks out the 'weak elements' in a particular workplace, punishing only those already prone to stress. Drawing together the various themes of this chapter and the previous one, we can see that – as with all aspects of job stress – the issue of personality is much more complicated than that, even leaving aside the crucial role of 'job fit'.

It seems likely that Jeffrey Gray and his colleagues – following the lead of the pioneer of behaviourism in this country, H. J. Eysenck – have correctly identified a trait they call 'neuroticism' – i.e. a tendency to react over-emotionally and then have difficulty in calming down again, which many people inherit, but to varying degrees. This tendency readily to go into and then stay in a state of high nervous reaction undoubtedly affects the amount of change and demand at work which a particular person can cope with, without becoming ill. We know that introversion predisposes people to act so as to avoid punishment rather than to gain reward. Someone with an introverted and 'neurotic' personality is undoubtedly more likely to appraise job challenges as potential threats – and we know that these kind of appraisals can lead, over long periods, to stress and illness.

On the other hand, if an individual is in a job which doesn't meet their own inherited preference for stimulation (their 'sensation-seeking' level), this too will represent a source of stress. And we know that tough-minded extroverts can gallop ambitiously into high blood pressure and heart attacks. However, it seems likely that many of these apparently dynamic individuals are in fact concealing neurotic anxieties and distresses which are part of the reason for their driven behaviour in the first place. High emotionality and anxiety are associated with heart disease but, as Dr Clive Wood has pointed out recently in *New Scientist*, *low* emotionality is typical of people who seem to react to certain stresses by contracting cancer (this is mirrored coincidentally by the unusually *low* levels of cholesterol found in their blood).

It seems likely that there are optimal levels of tendency to emotionality – not too much, not too little – which thankfully most of us inherit anyway. But it has been suggested that people who are at either end of the spectrum might well gain from treatment programmes. These can help those people who now tend to suffer from anxiety and depression to understand better how to evaluate their own emotional response and also help those who presently inhibit their emotionality to become more insightful at recognising their own hidden feelings and expressing them more assertively.

Similarly, individuals who are bringing behaviour patterns which they first developed as children to their adult jobs are likely to create stresses for themselves in their work – but not if, as we have seen, they are given some chance to gain insight into their maladaptive behaviour. Then they are more than usually motivated to develop effective, efficient and self-satisfying approaches to their work. They will thus be *less* rather than more likely to succumb to externally generated stress at work.

As we have also seen, some people – the unassertive, obsessive, ambitious, and risk-seeking – are particularly vulnerable in their own way to the three major potential sources of stress at work, relationships, responsibility, and changing conditions. But, here again – with help and recognition and advice – they can quickly gain some insight into the ineffectiveness of some of their favourite if misguided techniques for trying to cope with tasks.

Finally, all these factors – inherited constitution, early experience, and later experiences as people encounter the realities of school, friends and employment – come together to determine whether we tend to be pessimists or optimists, and whether we tend to assume that we can cope or not. It is known that some people learn helplessness as they grow up. They come to believe that calm, reasoned actions will *not* be effective in gaining their ends or responding to changes in their home or work situations. This 'can't cope' response is clearly associated with depression and anxiety and, in a recent study, people who described themselves in this way were shown often to have suppressed function of the immune system. Along with good 'job fit', *attitude* is probably the most important single personality factor in determining whether people are highly prone to stress at work or not. Happily it is also the most amenable to conscious effort on the part of individuals.

Winning through winning

Dr Steven Greer, who carried out some of the pioneering work on breast cancer and depression that we described earlier, discovered that – among women diagnosed as suffering from cancer – the ones who responded with a positive determination to conquer the illness and tried to take action were significantly more likely to be free of symptoms five years later.

The psychologist Susan Kobasa in the USA has made a study of individuals with unusually low levels of reported stress and low levels of illness. She calls them 'hardy personalities'. Typically, these people say that their life and work are coherent and make sense to them – they feel committed to what they do and in control of how they do it. They tend to welcome change, seeing it as a challenge and an opportunity. In a sense they are the charismatic, purposeful kind of people that many driven, ambitious workers pretend to be, and most of us wouldn't mind being either. As a group, these 'hardy personalities' sound daunting, and any of us might be forgiven if we don't feel up to adopting all of their well-balanced and effective strategies for dealing with life.

Still, we can all consciously decide that we *will* take a more positive attitude to ourselves and our work. But to do this in an effective way we must first identify just what are the stresses built into the jobs we do, and then decide what actions can be taken to remedy them – both by individual employees and, perhaps even more importantly, by employers.

CHAPTER FIVE

Filers, foremen and fitters

A major source of satisfaction or stress for people at work lies in how much they are asked to do and how much control they have over the way they do it. For example, one way of understanding the Type As' problems is to see them as misguided attempts to keep complete control over all the elements in their jobs by taking on excessive numbers of tasks. It's not just busy Type As who face problems of control, however. All sorts of people, with varying amounts of responsibility, can encounter difficulties over the amount of control they have over their jobs.

Lack of opportunity for control or low 'decision latitude' is clearly related to depression at work. People will accept occasional high levels of demand quite happily if they feel competent, confident and skilful in what they are doing.

Workers of fairly low status are often stressed by the amounts they have to do which are imposed on them by other people. In this chapter, we will look at three very different groups of workers – clerical workers involved in processing information, supervisors and foremen, and production-line workers. All of them can face problems of control in their work.

Filers

For many clerical workers, it is not possible to anticipate or determine the amount of work they will have to do at any one time, particularly when they have to respond immediately to demands made on them by the other people with whom they have to deal as part of their job. This can give rise to periods with too little to do, which can be boring, followed by others with too much to do, when it is important to keep a cool head to avoid feelings of panic.

For Cathy, a marketing assistant at a Manchester chemicals company, pressure is an integral part of the work in a sales office.

> We are here as a back-up team for the sales managers out on the road. We work closely with Production – we have to, because we take the orders from the customers. We can promise them any delivery [date] but if Production can't make it, then we might as well just not take the order. So the main thing is really to make sure that the customer's happy and to make sure Production's happy.
>
> The main problem with trying to keep everybody happy is that you get a telephone call, you get a query from a customer, then before you've got time to sort it out, the phone rings again. . . . This goes on all day, and if you haven't got the time to sort it out, then you've got hundreds of problems building up on your desk. So you've got to categorise them into which you think you must give the highest priority to, and that is the most difficult thing for us to do, because obviously every order is important.
>
> It can be terribly stressful when you've got a lot to do. But on the other hand, when there isn't a lot coming in, when you've got holidays and people aren't there and the phones are very quiet – that can be as stressful as having too much to do. It's just trying to find the happy medium where you've got just enough to do to keep you going and keep the pattern going all day.

Cathy finds the going sometimes gets tough, but the periods when she is under pressure never last so long that things become unmanageable. As such, these periods are more stimulating than stressful. Cathy manages to cope with her job since she is never too seriously overloaded for too long, and she has the comforting knowledge in the back of her mind that she can fall back on help from her colleagues if things ever do seem likely to slip out of control.

In some industries, pressure on employees has been increased as a result of staff cut-backs. The Inland Revenue has been particularly hard hit by cuts in recent years and the effects are keenly felt by its employees. Professor Cary Cooper has estimated that, as a group, tax officers are now about three times more likely to show signs of mental ill-health – like anxiety, depression and psychosomatic illness – than the average. Clerical staff in certain sections of the Inland Revenue are faced with enormous backlogs of work which they know they cannot catch up with.

They cannot find the time to bring themselves up to date with changes in the tax legislation, and pressure to deal with as many individual cases as fast as possible means that staff are sometimes conscious of making errors but do not have the time to deal with a particular case properly. Having more work than they can cope with, and being aware of sometimes doing a less than good job through lack of time, puts paid to much hope of job satisfaction. Members of the public, made to wait inordinate lengths of time for their cases to be dealt with, add to the pressure by showing understandable impatience. If tax officers take a holiday, they do so in the knowledge that their work, left unattended, will have increased in volume by the time they come back.

Management can also be a problem. Some managers are unsympathetic to the problems faced by their staff. Decisions are made at a remote distance, which makes many tax officers feel a frustrating lack of control over their own work. Lack of control through being unable to deal with excessive quantities of work and through being excluded from decision-making about the way in which the work is done is probably at the root of much of the stress currently felt by tax officers.

Peter is a higher grade tax officer in Manchester. He has worked for the Inland Revenue for sixteen years and finds that his job has changed a lot in that time.

The basic problem is lack of staff at the moment. Although dealing with 500 tax-payers, as I do, doesn't sound like very much, they are extremely complicated. You can spend two or three days on one item of post for one tax-payer when there aren't even 500 days in the year. You need time to assimilate knowledge of tax changes but you don't get time. . . .

When I first started in the Revenue in 1969 the whole way the job was done was different. The job then was enjoyable because you were actually helping people. Now the job is to deal with the case as quickly as you can, get it off your desk as quickly as possible, not to make sure that the thing is correct. So you're having to put out work which you know isn't correct. . . .

What seems to be a general problem throughout the Revenue is this lack of involvement, the lack of consultation about the way the job is done. Rather than consult, changes within the office are dictated. So of course people don't feel involved in the way their job is done, they don't feel particularly involved in any decision-making process. . . .

Gail, a tax officer in a smaller tax office also in Manchester, finds she has similar difficulties stemming from being overloaded.

When the post builds up to a point where it is now, it's very difficult to cope. It's sometimes a feeling of panic because people . . . want to know why you've not dealt with their letters. They don't understand that there aren't enough people to actually do the job, not enough hours in the day sometimes to get through it. Some people get abusive. They accuse us of mistreating them personally. . . .

Some managers do take our problems seriously but I do know that there are others who don't. It's not very good for morale when you know that some of our senior managers think that we're simply intrinsically lazy. They think that we can cope with whatever we're given, and should cope with whatever we're given, no matter what stresses that puts on us personally.

Professor Cary Cooper has devised the following checklist for office workers: Do any of the following apply to your work organisation? Answer Yes or No to each of the questions below:

* Decisions and changes are regularly made from above without informing workers.
* Management doesn't seem to understand workers' problems.
* To cope with their job, workers regularly have to work extra hours, sometimes weekends.

* Work regularly interferes with the personal and family life of workers.
* There is a lot of irritability at work, backbiting between colleagues and bad temper with subordinates.

If you answered Yes to even one of these questions, it's a warning that you or your colleagues are working in potentially stressful conditions and may already be showing signs of stress. When faced with problems like these, managers often blame hard times or cuts in spending, but often the roots of these problems lie in poor management. Managers who don't recognise that stress problems are real certainly won't try to do anything about them.

If you are able to set your own work pace and allocate your own efforts, here are some well verified tips for minimising the stresses and strains of the nine to five and becoming both more relaxed and effective in the process.

Every day, at the start of the day:

1 Define your objectives – all of them. This sounds obvious, but a great many people never sit down and think for a moment what it is that they really want to achieve.

2 Arrange your objectives into three groups of priorities of action: must be done today, medium-term action (better done tomorrow) and very long-term aims.

3 Arrange today's action list in order of your reluctance to get on with each item.

4 Do the things you'd rather put off *first*.

5 Reward yourself with a sociable non-working lunch – preferably taken away from your workplace. If you can take some exercise go for a stroll or even a short jog or swim.

6 Either work through your list (you can amend it as you go through the day) until it's time to go home or – if things go more quickly and easily than you expected, either go home if you're allowed to, or simply relax. Don't use the opportunity to make more work for yourself.

7 If an item keeps turning up on your daily list for more than two or three days *cross it off*. You know unconsciously that it doesn't really matter.

8 If you're slipping behind with your work, or finding it constantly arduous and demanding, stop and take a good look at the whole situation. It may be time for you to take a break, or talk to your supervisor about the amount of work you're being asked to do.

9 Don't accept that you're paid to worry or 'you shouldn't have come into the kitchen if the fire's too hot'.

10 Stress is your personal response to trying to do the *wrong* job. This might be either because of the way you're doing it or what's being asked of you. Your supervisors should be willing to discuss this with you – without blame – it's to their benefit too.

Foremen

Supervisors and foremen have more autonomy than many clerical workers but, combined with this, they have to cope with more responsibility. Dave, a shift leader in a chemicals factory, enjoys the control he has in his job, but at times finds the responsibility a worry.

> Basically, I'm in charge of running the reactors, monitoring everything that goes on, and making a product from start to finish, with the back-up of a manager on days. It's down to me on nights, weekends and whatever else. I've got a lot of autonomy. We're here seven days a week. Office staff, managers, they're only here during the day. Any other time – decisions to make are mine, and anything that goes wrong, it's up to me to try and get it fixed as fast as possible.
>
> It can cause quite a bit of stress if things are going wrong and you can't really find what's wrong. A lot of the time we're just monitoring, so there's very little to do at all. It can get extremely boring one minute and a mad-house the next. Everything can go wrong at once. . . .
>
> I get more pressure from underneath. There's very little pressure from above, as I say, most of it is left to me to run anyway. We work in a team, we discuss things together. It's not a case of me just saying, 'Right you do that.' We come

to a conclusion through asking all around, instead of me
just bossing them about.

I'm easy going. I don't get upset very easily. I very rarely
lose my temper. Otherwise you just couldn't do it.

Although he likes to work as a member of a team and to
consult the men responsible to him, Dave is himself responsible
for making decisions and, of course, for the effects that these
may have. This control can be a source of some anxiety at times
but, more importantly, it gives him involvement and satisfaction
in his work. The demand which his job makes on him is variable,
things can change from boredom one moment to pandemonium
the next.

Middle supervisors and foremen face an inherent difficulty in
their jobs as a result of their position in the organisational hierarchy. Such people suffer frequently from the problems of
conflicting job demands – on the one hand trying to please and
win the co-operation of the workers whom they supervise, and
on the other trying to comply with the demands made by senior
management. They are caught in the middle. In his book *The
Stress Check* Cary Cooper writes that 'the organisational role
which is at a boundary – that is between departments, or between
the company and the outside world – is, by definition, one of
high role conflict'.

Research has found that such positions are usually highly
stressful. People with high role conflict have been found to have
lower job satisfaction and higher job-related tension. Across a
number of different industries, middle managers and supervisors
are prone to high levels of stress illness. Fred, an ex-foreman at
Ford's, encountered many problems attached to his role in that
organisation but in general enjoyed coping with them. Some of
his colleagues, he remembers, were less successful.

Twenty-two years ago, I became a general foreman of
running a shift. And, of course, this gives you quite a lot of
scope. You are helping, in a way, to make decisions. You
don't make the major ones of course, and you don't negotiate wages or anything like that. But you can have a great
deal of say as to how your shift of men operate. Now there's
only one problem there – you are piggy-in-the-middle. On

the one hand you've got to satisfy the aspirations of your lads as far as their working conditions are concerned, on the other, you've got the management's targets and how they want things to proceed.

He ends on a positive note, reflecting his own positive attitude to life and work.

To me it was a challenge which I enjoyed – to see just how much I could get away with, as it were, in the middle, between management and the lads.

Five key points for supervisors

1 Define your objectives clearly to yourself. Don't give yourself mixed objectives. For a given task, decide whether your primary responsibility is to the management above you or to your subordinates. Make your decision clear to your subordinates.
2 Delegate tasks which you know you could do but which the people who work for you should be capable of doing (even if they don't do it quite as well as you).
3 When you delegate, don't interfere with the person who is doing the task. Once you give them the job it should be entirely their responsibility. Wait till they have finished and then tell them whether they have done it properly or not.
4 Don't be afraid to tell people they've got it wrong but don't blame, and only reprimand if you're absolutely sure the person has the wrong approach. (This should be very rarely.)
5 Whenever you can, give feedback to your subordinates on their performance and tell them when you appreciate their work, but don't be lavish. The praise of superiors – if given in a balanced way – makes the sun shine all day.

. . . and fitters

For shop-floor workers in general, there is a low level of responsibility combined with minimal control over the job they do and very often a consequent lack of involvement. Keith is a manual worker in a Manchester factory who spends all his working day filling sacks with polystyrene chips. The work is physically demanding and physically unpleasant in that it requires him to work in extremely noisy, dirty conditions, breathing chemical fumes and obliged by law to wear protective earmuffs. Though it is physically demanding, the job is most of the time mindlessly monotonous. Keith does it only for the money (and he considers this to be inadequate), which he needs to support his family. He gets no satisfaction from his work and spends his long twelve-hour shift waiting for it to end so that he can go home.

> I've got to make sure the machine's set up right and make sure that everything's in working order. I'm stuck on that, lifting 25-kilo sacks, and I've got to stack them up forty bags high.... That's my job. If something does go wrong and I can't put it right, then I've got to go and see the shift leader who has a look at it himself.
>
> You've got to stick it for the twelve hours. You get your breaks in between, but you've still got to work in there and you've got to wear protective earmuffs all day which aren't very comfortable. It's noisy, dusty, dirty.... Sometimes it does get interesting but 90 per cent of the time it's the same job, just standing all day doing nothing.
>
> The only good thing about the job is going home at night time at seven o'clock. When seven o'clock comes we all make a rush for the gate and out we go back home. There's no job satisfaction for me. It's just a job – just money.

In the case of many assembly-line workers, this lack of involvement can become total alienation. It is generally thought that paced work presents greater problems than unpaced work. When the speed at which people work is set by the speed of a production line, it becomes impossible to break off even to go to the lavatory. Despite developments in robotics and computer-controlled processes, many people still find themselves doing mind-numbing jobs, much better suited to machines than to thinking human beings. In such cases, job satisfaction is virtually zero and many people only remain through fear of the dole queue.

Steve is a production-line worker at Ford's in Dagenham.

> My particular job is fitting front seats. So as the car arrives, you pick up one seat, throw it to the other side of the car, pick up the next seat, put it in the car and then fit it. By the time you've done that, the next car's arrived, so then you go back and do the next repeat process. If you stop for a moment to, say, blow your nose, you'll find that the car is down further than your work station, so then you've got to try and work twice as hard to catch back up because once it goes out of your work station, it's gone, and the foreman will be down there asking you why it's been missed and possibly discipline you.
>
> Again, if you wanted to, say, go to the loo, we have to ask the foreman for permission. First of all you've got to try and find him and you can't get off the job to find him because you're tied to the job.
>
> More often than not, people feel that they are no more than a robot. They're timed in an inhumane way by the work standards engineer. He will time a man and say, 'Right, it only takes a certain amount of time for you to, say, put four twists on a screw, so it will only take a certain amount of time to put ten twists on a bolt', and then that is set and that's what you are expected to perform to on every single job, and so is every single other person who comes on that job. So people feel that they are being treated just like a robot, and they've got no control over that whatsoever. You try and turn yourself off, you try and not think because there's nothing to concentrate on, so each minute seems like an hour and you're just wishing every hour away.

Steve's colleague Jim found that the mindless repetitiveness of his job on the line caused him to make mistakes while being totally unaware of doing so:

> I had to put a certain measure of oil in the engine. I had to turn a dial and press a button like a petrol pump and it would shoot the required amount of oil into the engine.

The engines would come past me, probably about ninety an hour.

On this particular occasion, the foreman came to me and said that they had four engines with no oil in them and he wanted an explanation. I told him that it was most probably that the machine had malfunctioned because I was convinced that I'd put oil in those engines. In the afternoon, he came steaming back to me and told me that they had twenty engines with no oil and he wanted an explanation. Not only had they twenty engines with no oil but he had five with double oil. I couldn't give an explanation for that, and I didn't do it on purpose. As far as I was concerned I was doing my job conscientiously. But the thing is, I couldn't cope with the boredom.

In the Ford assembly plant at Dagenham, tea breaks have understandably become crucially important islands of recreation in the working day. 'Tea-taster' is a formal and elected position, recognised by both the unions and employers. Tea-tasters officially declare the tea to be adequate. This system has developed in order to prevent the quality of the tea from becoming the focus of disputes, as individuals may declare it to be undrinkable.

Blue-collar workers suffer significantly higher rates of stress-related disease than do white-collar workers. A popular myth persists that it is high-powered executives who have to contend with the highest levels of stress. In fact, it appears that the level of stress-related illness correlates very closely with the status level of workers' jobs, and that it is the people at the bottom who are by far the worst off. This may well be due in large part to the lack of control which they have over their work, and the lack of interest and purpose which they find in it.

A number of studies have been done on this. For instance, one American study found that the incidence rate of first disabling coronary heart disease was two and a half times greater amongst skilled manual workers than amongst executive grades, and that the rate increased inversely with occupational grade. A similar relationship was found in cases of myocardial infarction among industrial workers.

It is argued that the existence of such jobs, in which work is often paced by a machine and which combine low responsibility, low status, low control, low variety and no opportunity for self-motivation, is a necessary implication of unskilled manual labour used with modern production technology. But do things really need to be this bad?

The organisation of the Trebor factory at Colchester has been devised to try to avoid many of these problems and to promote involvement and job satisfaction amongst the people who work there. The factory is run without charge hands or supervisors. The work is carried out by small groups of five to ten people who work together without a leader and have the responsibility of meeting their week's target in the way they see best. Members of each group organise job rotation, relief and service, quality control, supplies of raw materials and the delivery of the product to the warehouse. As a result, production levels are on a par with those at other, more traditionally organised Trebor factories, but the attitude of the employees towards their work is significantly better.

The aim, as Niall Christie, works manager at the Colchester factory, explains, is 'to push the decision-making process down to the lowest levels where the information is available, to stretch people as much as possible and to utilise all the innate skills which they have'. The objective is to get people to solve their own problems, so there is a minimal hierarchy. As far as possible there is a single status amongst all employees. There is no clocking on, everyone queues in the same restaurant, everyone has equal claim on car parking space, everyone is paid monthly at one of two rates of pay. People can take as many breaks as they like, as long as they meet their required production level at the end of the week. The organisation of the factory is designed to give people freedom, variety, involvement and satisfaction in their work, and it does appear to be very successful.

The problems attached to it are felt not so much by the shop-floor workers as by the handful of managers, who are obliged to trust people to make their own decisions and get on with the job. Managers spend a lot of time on the shop floor, talking to people about their work, rather than simply handing down orders as in a traditionally run factory.

Trebor's employees make it clear that they enjoy this way of working. They value the responsibility, freedom and control which they are given, feel respected and valued themselves, and enjoy the variety of changing jobs among themselves. Here are some typical comments:

I feel very involved because if I want to start off I can go in the press room where the mints are actually pressed, I can run that part of it, and then I can come out on the floor and run a machine, or sit on the end of the machine and pack them, so you go through the whole process of actually starting off with them being pressed to the finished product going on the belt and being overwrapped.

Us all working together is what our company is all about. People being able to work on their own initiative and getting on and doing the job without having somebody standing over them saying you must do this and you must do that.

It's a great job. Other factories are too out of date in comparison to this factory in methods. Here you've got no foremen, you've got decent people to work with, you can go for a drink, go for a smoke, nobody really bothers as long as the process is running well.

The Medical Research Council was interested in the effects that the organisation of the Trebor factory at Colchester would have on employees' attitude towards work and the company, and conducted a three-year research project from the time that work at the factory started. As Niall Christie says, the research findings

demonstrated fairly conclusively that the attitude of people towards the work and the complexity of the task, and the general satisfaction, is significantly higher than it is at our Chesterfield factory, which is organised along very traditional hierarchical lines. Not only is it better than Chesterfield, it's significantly better than the norms of British industry generally.

The organisation of workers into semi-autonomous work groups is not unique to Trebor. Studies done in a sewing factory in the 1940s by Coch and French found that greater participation resulted in higher productivity, greater job satisfaction, lower staff turnover and better relationships between boss and subordinates. Subsequent research has confirmed this. A number of organisations have introduced semi-autonomous work groups in order to increase the involvement of their employees.

Volvo's project is perhaps the most famous. People there work in teams and train the new members of their teams themselves. Jobs are rotated and people work with no overtime payments until their previously agreed quota is met. If they finish early, there are various facilities like a sauna and swimming pool at the plant, which they can use. It seems a very long way from the clock-watching and mass rush for the gates typical of the traditional factory.

This form of work organisation is still fairly limited in this country and is often seen as a rather trendy experiment instituted by a benevolent but possibly slightly irresponsible management. Nonetheless, such experiments, which attempt to increase participation amongst workers, are becoming more common. The new approach is to move away from the traditional production line, in which every individual is a tiny cog in an enormous wheel, towards a set-up in which every worker is part of the whole production process and is motivated by group co-operation and pride in the finished product, rather than simply by management coercion.

Checklist for manual workers

* Do you get enough variety in your job?
* Are you given any opportunity to make decisions about your work?
* Are you ever expected to solve problems that arise for yourself?
* Are you able to take reasonable breaks when you like?
* Does your job make good use of the skills which have?

[86] **How to survive the 9 to 5**
* Do you feel stretched by the demands which your job makes on you?
* Do you feel valued and respected by your managers?
* Do you feel any sense of pride in the product you make?

If the answer to any one of these questions is No, then there is a potential source of stress in the way your factory is run. It's time you and your co-workers did something about it!

CHAPTER SIX

Relationships

> In my department there are six people who are afraid of me, and one small secretary who is afraid of all of us. I have one other person working for me who is not afraid of anyone, not even me, and I would fire him quickly, but I'm afraid of him.

So says Joseph Heller in *Something Happened*, a tongue-in-cheek but penetrating novel about stress in the workplace. How true this can be was demonstrated by J. R. P. French and R. D. Caplan in *The Failure of Success*, who found that mistrust of colleagues is linked to 'high role ambiguity' leading to 'psychological strain in the form of low job satisfaction and to feelings of job-related threat to one's well-being'. They defined poor relationships as characterised by 'low trust, low supportiveness, and low interest in listening to and trying to deal with problems that confront the organisational member'.

Man is a social animal, and there is no automatic cut-off of his social instincts as he enters the factory gate. Behavioural scientists have believed for some time that the relationships we have at work are a major factor in job satisfaction – and hence the amount of stress generated by our jobs.

Despite having strong suspicions that this 'social network' is important to both individual and organisational health, scientists have done very little research into the area of relationships at work. There is, however, evidence from research into the stresses of life *outside* work which can help us to understand how and why good relationships can be so important.

A major study of men of Japanese origin, living in Japan, Hawaii and California, has shown what seems to be a clear link between coronary heart disease and lack of good relationships with people in their immediate community. The researchers found that Japanese living in California suffered from about twice the level of coronary heart disease as their peer group in Japan, even taking into account all the known risk factors such as smoking and diet. Their conclusion was that these differences may simply be caused by the different lifestyles in the two countries. In America, the Japanese had adopted the American way of life with mobile, independent nuclear families while in Japan they clung to the tradition of extended family groups and paternalistic companies. The study concluded that the American Japanese didn't have adequate social support to cope with the amount of stress they encountered.

Another interesting report came from a researcher who looked at unemployment among blue-collar men. She found that the men who had a lot of social support took the loss of their jobs less badly than those who were loners at work. The socially supported men had lower cholesterol levels in their blood, fewer peptic ulcers and less illness generally than their friendless peers.

This study is confirmed by many recent surveys of Britain's increasing number of unemployed. Many report feeling depression at the loss of the companionship of their workmates, and they regain their well-being if they become involved with supportive groups that operate outside the workplace. In a later chapter we will meet Jim, an unemployed council worker, who goes so far as to say that his unemployment is more fulfilling to him than his previous employment because he has better relationships with the people he meets in community groups than he ever did with his workmates.

Manchester workers reported, in a recent survey carried out by the University of Manchester's Institute of Science and Technology (UMIST), that the second greatest source of job satisfaction to them came from their colleagues (the first was the level of supervision they received). The nearer retirement the workers were, the more social satisfaction they obtained from their jobs – which makes the 'early retirement' encouraged by many firms seem particularly callous, the UMIST researchers conclude.

Good relationships lead to good feelings about self and work. On the other hand, of course, bad relationships can be very destructive.

And an interesting footnote from the world of laboratory rats. It has been found that rats given unexpected electric shocks had high rates of peptic ulcers if they were on their own, but low rates of ulceration if the shocks happened while they were in the company of their litter mates. Not quite a situation we might meet at work but you can see the parallels!

Relationships with colleagues

Office politics and the rivalry of our colleagues can be a source of considerable stress to us, but it can also be our colleagues who are the source of most of the social support we receive at work. As the study of Manchester workers shows, we need to like our colleagues in order to get more satisfaction out of our jobs. But more than that, they can save our lives – it has been found that our colleagues can mitigate the wear and tear caused to us by high-stress jobs.

One of the best studies that has been done recently on high-stress jobs is one on the job that must be one of the most highly pressurised of all – that of air-traffic controller. Air-traffic controllers are often thought of as solitary animals, eyes glued to a screen of tiny blips, and having the psychologically fascinating ability to listen to two conversations simultaneously while replying to a third. Legend has it that they are unsociable, independent and burn out young – an image assiduously fostered by airport disaster films. The 'unsociable and independent' parts have clearly been shown to be untrue. John, an air-traffic controller at a major British airport, prizes the great amount of support he gets from his friends and team mates.

> I think that having the support of the other controllers around you is a very important part of the job. One always assumes that if one of your mates gets into trouble, he will ask the others to help him. I would do exactly that if I was going under and was not able to cope. I would call for assistance from my friends, the blokes I can trust. There's a lot of trust in controlling. You've got to trust the pilots, but particularly you've got to trust that the other members of your team are going to give you aeroplanes in the right place,

doing the right thing, so that you can get on and do your part of the job. If one controller couldn't trust another controller, I should imagine the amount of stress he's subjected to must be about ten times the amount that he actually suffers at the moment.

The study shows that John is quite right. An air-traffic controller's job is one of high stress, but the effects are lessened by a strong support network amongst his colleagues. A controller with poor social skills, or one who can't or won't rely on the support of his colleagues, is at far more risk of stress-related disorders, particularly heart attacks. John finds that he enjoys being part of a support network so much that he rates it one of the greatest satisfactions of his work.

The stress of the job is knowing that you've got to get it right all the time and that there are a lot of people depending upon you, that there are a lot of things that you've got to cope with. There are a lot of variables that the controller has got to keep in his mind and he's got to keep adjusting those. Aeroplanes are coming at him all the time and he's got to do something with them.

A controller needs to be more of an extrovert than an introvert. He has to work as a part of a team. It's no good people doing their own thing and ignoring what's going on around them. They have to make decisions in concert with the other members of the team – that is the controllers around them, controllers in adjacent centres and of course the pilots of the aircraft concerned.

Although team work is more or less essential to well-being in John's high-pressure job, it can still be of very great importance in less frantic jobs.

Gail, the tax officer we met in the last chapter, is under some pressure at the moment because her office is very short-staffed. Her satisfaction in doing a good job has been severely curtailed as she finds she no longer has the time she would like to devote to each of her cases. And in this time of pressure, Gail finds that the support of her colleagues, both sharing the work and giving emotional backing, is vitally important to her. 'In the office we try to cope by getting on with each other. There's no point in taking it out on your colleagues. I suppose it's something like the feeling of the Blitz. Everybody's in it together, we're all in the same situation and that's how we cope – by staying happy with each other.'

Air hostesses also find that relationships are an integral part of their job. They have to relate to their clients – the airline passengers. Karen and Kaye, two stewardesses with a major carrier, find that this relationship does not always go as smoothly as they would like. But then they can rely on the other members of the cabin staff to help them along.

> Generally the passengers are nice to us. Occasionally there's a difficult case, but though this person might be being difficult with you, you've got to think about what might have gone on in their life prior to meeting you. They might have had some terrible incident at home. I don't personally let it get to me. In our job, a lot of this is to do with nerves and tension and the best thing is if we look happy and confident – I'm sure that helps.

> When there's lots of things that have gone wrong on a particular flight and there seems to be a high percentage of obnoxious people, I often find that other members of the crew have experienced them as well. You can go in the galley where no one can see you and discuss it among yourselves and then it all seems better.

Relationships with subordinates

One of the main stresses on managers these days, reports tend to show, is that managing *things* is not enough any more, they must manage *people* in a participatory manner. They are expected to create 'teams' and foster a team spirit. In fact, subordinates have been shown to prefer a person-oriented manager to a task-oriented one – except in specific circumstances where achieving a set goal demands tight structuring of their work.

Chris, an airline pilot, finds that one of his major problems is finding a balance between the two styles. His job is to get the plane safely from A to B. But the plane is full of passengers who have to be kept happy by the cabin crew, who in turn have to be kept happy by him! He has to be largely person-oriented in his management style, and he confesses that he occasionally finds it a strain.

> Everybody thinks that flying aeroplanes is stressful. It really isn't, because the flight itself can be controlled mainly by computer. We do the take-off and landing, and most of the rest of the time it is just computer-controlled. The real stress comes in another area and that is to do with crew co-operation. Being able to fly from A to B is very largely now an automated process. The thing we can't automate is someone having a small trauma about something that is personally very important to them. And so a very large part of my role is associated with ensuring that whatever problems they've got are left very firmly at home and that while they're acting as a crew member, they're under the total control of the senior cabin crew member who is acting under the guidance of the captain.
>
> To be a successful captain, you have got to be essentially a little extrovert. You have got to be a man-manager or woman-manager, and you have to be able to assess people's personal problems before they become so great that they start to interfere with their day-to-day work.
>
> One has to look at what each individual member of the crew is doing and to ensure that each knows that his job is worthwhile and appreciated by the captain. To succeed in my job, I have to bring out the best of every individual member, draw them all together and draw co-operation out of them, because I know that our very lives might depend on it. Essentially the whole thing is getting the crew together and working as a team. That's the magic word, the team.

Reading between the lines of what Chris says, in spite of his mild grousing, he finds that his person-oriented management style works. He pulls his team together and can give himself a pat on the back whenever he smooths over a potential upset.

A study by R. D. Caplan of NASA personnel found that good work relations, particularly with subordinates, acted as a sort of 'buffer' against stress. A manager who felt uncertain of his position in the organisation was more likely to suffer from high blood cholesterol levels or high blood pressure if he also had poor relations with his subordinates.

Relationships with bosses

We have seen that office relationships are at their best when one has colleagues to call on, and when one works for a person-oriented boss. A vivid illustration of what life can be like for a subordinate who has a poor relationship with a boss comes from Roma, a secretary in an engineering firm. Her boss was so task-oriented that she came to feel that she was little more than an extension of one of the machines in the office.

> The pressure was on really right from the beginning. And relationships in the department were very difficult. The manager who ran the department wasn't relating to other people in the department properly, and they weren't relating to him. He steamed ahead and seemed to do everything and take everything on himself. Nobody could ever help him. And I was his secretary.
>
> I found myself not doing the normal duties of a senior secretary within a department, which would be to handle all the admin. I was to concentrate on the word processor. I got very, very tired and stressed and had to consult a doctor who told me to ease off. I was working horrific hours, some-times more overtime than straight time, because that was the way my boss worked. He got in at seven-thirty in the morn-ing and he would go on till ten-thirty, eleven o'clock at night, all weekends. I've even known him to be there all night.

The effect of this bad relationship with her superior was not simply to provide Roma with an unnecessary source of stress, but also to cut her off from her colleagues. If she had been working as part of a team, she would at least have had the support of her peers.

> I came to feel like a zombie eventually. I used to ask him to explain things to me and he'd say, 'You don't need to know that, just type it.' So I couldn't function in my job as a person any longer. I was just there as an extension of the

machine. To work like that with a machine, I think some-thing happens to one emotionally. You're not getting any human responses. If you give out you've got to get in. And I wasn't getting anything back from whatever I did.

I used to get very upset about all this, and I couldn't turn to anybody else. There was nobody I could relate to in my work. There was no connection between me and anybody else. Just me and the machine, endlessly, sometimes fourteen hours a day. I was becoming ill, I didn't know what was happening, I was becoming more and more isolated, and feeling that nobody understood.

First of all I had stomach pains, which I was told was stress, so I tried to back off a bit. But then the pressure was kept up and gradually I became more and more like a zombie. I began having dreams that I was in a concentration camp with a Gestapo officer standing over me hitting me with a gun butt, and I was saying, 'I'll carry on, I'll carry on.' And that was how I was going, just carrying on, carrying on.

The manager who I worked for was replaced. In fact, my prayers were answered [but] it was at that moment that I became ill, because I went to the new manager and said, 'Am I going to be your secretary now?' and he said, 'No, we want you on that machine.' That's when I went to lunch and couldn't walk in a straight line when I came back.

I started to fall over to the right. My hands became diffi-cult . . . my feet became numb, and the left-hand side of my face became numb. My main feeling was just utter help-lessness because I was not in control of my body any longer. It was a very frightening time, because nobody understood. I eventually ended up seeing a psychiatrist who said that my motor nervous system had failed.

I went home sick and stayed sick. I've been sick now for three years. I feel I'm getting a lot better and I'll soon be able to work again, but I have to find something different. I'll never, never be a secretary again and I will never operate a word processor again, of that I'm utterly sure.

But what Roma experienced is not an isolated case. Cary

Cooper has just done a study of word processor operators and secretaries. He found that being undervalued and not supported by the boss was one of the main causes of poor mental health. In fact, it may even be that the reported increase in miscarriages among VDU operators is a result of how they are managed, and other stresses of the job, rather than radiation exposure.

Relationships across the organisation's boundaries

In addition to the relationships we have looked at with fellow employees, there is another important type of relationship which can be either a source of stress or satisfaction – and that is with clients or customers.

We have already met two air hostesses who say that the passengers can be a source of stress to them. It is clear from what they say that successfully coping with a passenger's problem is a source of satisfaction to them.

> I think you've got to be pretty placid. You can't get very excitable. You've also got to be outgoing, in a balanced way – not a crazy extrovert. You've got to be able to deal with illnesses, so you've got to be caring as well. And of course you're always aware of your emergency procedures. You've got to be able to cope in dealing with anything like that, so in that sense you've got to keep calm and level-headed. You've got to be able to communicate well with people and make them feel happy. I suppose it is our job to do that.

Kaye and Karen are lucky. Bill, the operator of a one-man bus in Stevenage, would have welcomed it if his passengers had made some demands of him. Instead, they paid him no attention at all – they treated him as a machine. He felt that when he got into his bus, he lost all personality and individual identity. He complained that the only time anyone paid him any attention was when they abused him – as though he were a faulty vending machine. Eventually Bill had a heart attack and was off work for a long time.

> I'm certainly convinced that a big factor contributing to that heart attack was the stress of the job. In my own garage

in the last two and a half years, there have been six heart attacks and, very sadly, two drivers have died. The passengers can't identify with an OMO [one-man-operated] driver. Quite often you're regarded as a retarded orang-outang. I've even had my wife get on a bus and walk straight past me. There's no recognition, you're simply part of a machine. Passengers' attitude towards drivers can be a very salient factor in stress conditions. . . . You're a non-person sitting in front of that wheel. . . . By the time you get home, you are absolutely tired out and very often family and wife can suffer because there's a fair unwinding process.

Like the air hostesses, Bill says that he can draw on the support of his colleagues, other one-man bus operators, to help him in his relationship problems with his passengers.

Among one-man-operated bus drivers, there's a unique camaraderie. We face common difficulties and dangers. We discuss it daily – at breaks, over coffee in the canteen. Talking among drivers about common problems is a safety valve. Although there'll be no real answer to a problem, at least for that given moment over a nice cup of coffee or tea, you feel, 'Well I'm not alone really. There's ninety-nine other drivers feeling exactly the same as me, facing the same problem.'

However, it is clear from what Bill says about the level of stress he felt he was under, and the comments he makes about the stress-illnesses suffered by other drivers, that this informal support network was not actually alleviating stress. It was more of a mutual grousing session – possibly even increasing the drivers' stress by increasing their awareness of the stressful situations without offering any remedies.

Going it alone

Some people who work alone feel acutely the need for social support. Consider the unfortunate lot of the dentist. He is a member of the caring professions, yet his patients often fear and hate him. Indeed he may have to cause them pain, something he may dread almost as much as his victims, as John, a London dentist explained.

> I think a lot of patients expect dentistry to be painful, and so a lot of patients [are] very nervous when they come in, and that imposes a lot more stress on the dentist because the patient is tense and so it tends automatically to make me tense . . . because their tolerance of dental procedures may be limited by their anxiety. . . . And so it takes more effort on the patient management side with nervous patients.

The dentist may feel he is inferior in status to other members of the medical profession. But, most importantly, dentists work alone for most of the time. Most have no one to share the burden with. They cannot discuss with an equal status colleague the moment-to-moment decisions about patient care. In the words of one: 'Many dentists don't relate closely to their nursing staff, they feel that there's a big gap between them and their nursing staff, and so I think for many dentists it is rather an isolated, lonely job. And there isn't anybody to moan to and help them to feel better at the end of the day.'

Although we may find the idea of a sad and lonely dentist vaguely amusing, we certainly shouldn't. Dentists commit suicide twice as often as the general population, and their life expectancy is horrifyingly low – around the late forties.

We can extrapolate from this sad state of affairs to the situation of our airline pilot, Chris. He seems to be saying that the pressures of managing his team mar what would otherwise be a pleasantly stress-free job. But would he be any better off if he flew an airliner manned only by robot cabin staff, with whom he didn't have to interact in any way? If he managed to eliminate his demanding but involving relationships with his crew, he would most likely find the actual task of flying the plane much more of a burden. With no one at his side to say, 'You're right!', 'Thank you', or 'Good landing!' the satisfaction he obtained from his job would decrease.

The organisation

Relationships with colleagues are not the only way in which we can gain emotional support from work. The organisation itself has an important role to play. Some companies, realising the gains that can result from meeting the needs of employees, are trying to be more supportive. As we said earlier, it has been known for at least forty years that greater participation at work leads to greater job satisfaction and higher productivity. The Swedes showed the way with the famous and highly successful scheme initiated by Volvo. Surprisingly few British companies have picked up on this – Trebor at Colchester being a notable exception.

It is hard to detail in limited space the numerous forms of group therapy that have sprung up in the last decade or so, aimed at helping people within organisations to develop social skills and good relationships. Some – such as nude encounter groups – are rather less popular than others!

The more conventional include:

Gestalt groups. Gestalt therapy aims to make people aware of themselves in any social situation – aware of the impact they have on others, of their personal style and how personal factors of which they may not be consciously aware can influence the outcome of any social encounter. Through self-awareness, and awareness of the situation, they can manipulate any encounter to good advantage.

Transactional analysis. Based on the work of Eric Berne and *The Games People Play*, this refers to the relation between 'ego-states' within a person. It says that we all flip between three states – child-adult-parent. We play a role which we feel will help us manipulate the best out of any situation. For example, we may play the child to avoid a justified telling-off – leaving the aggrieved party feeling frustrated and thwarted. Transactional analysis aims to teach us to understand and free ourselves from our 'games', so that personal interactions can take place on a calm, sensible and truly adult level.

Interpersonal skills training. This aims to help people to deal with clients. It is aimed at training people to deal with situations, not themselves. Police, for example, do not want to form a lationship with a 'client' – but they need to know how to defuse a potentially explosive situation. In training they are made to think about the responses that different forms of approach are likely to produce from someone.

An interesting addition to research on relationships is provided by an on-going American study of male blue-collar workers. So far it has shown that the support of wives and supervisors was a much more effective buffer against stress – measured by rates of angina, ulcers, skin itch, persistent cough and neurosis – than was the support of co-workers and friends and relatives. They believe that the reason is that a worker's supervisor is in the best position to help him deal with feelings of inadequacy at work, while his wife, by emphasising the rewards of family life and leisure, can help to put work problems in perspective.

So, although relationships at work are undeniably important, there is a good deal of conflict between the various researchers in the field about just how vital they are. One researcher has gone so far as to warn that inconsistencies between the studies that have been done 'argue against advocating social support as an all-purpose buffer against occupational stress ... what is more likely to emerge from future research is a more detailed specification of the circumstances under which social support does and does not ameliorate ... the effects of stress at work'. He says that much more research needs to be done.

In other words, if you like your colleagues, well and good. If not, it needn't be the end of the world. Not having good relationships may not be a stress to which you are particularly susceptible.

Checklist – does your organisation care for you?

* Can you discuss your performance with a superior without feeling under threat?
* Does your company provide access to an independent person with whom you can discuss your problems?
* Does your company have a health and welfare policy?
* Does it provide more than the legal minimum sickness/maternity/paternity leave?

[100] How to survive the 9 to 5

* Have you (or your boss) received any training in recognising sources of stress?
* Are you encouraged to develop personal interests or skills that are useful outside your present post?
* Does the company make clear what it expects of you and what it will give in return?
* Have you been told how to improve your promotion prospects?
* Are you actively encouraged to try for promotion?
* Are you able to participate in decisions that affect your work?
* Do your superiors insist on making regular operational decisions that you could easily make instead?
* Is there an effective grievance procedure?

Social support at work

The organisation can provide:

* Expert advice on problems
* Emotional support from counsellors, health and welfare officers
* Alternative non-stressful work
* Support for responsible jobs
* A sense of involvement

Informal groups can provide:

* A new source of ideas
* A shoulder to cry on
* Help with stressful work
* Shared responsibility
* A sense of belonging

(Derived from *The Stress Check* by Cary Cooper)

CHAPTER SEVEN

Keep smiling – the caring professions

There are times when smiling and being nice to people can be very hard work. Some jobs require people to constantly 'give' – they must always be cheerful, helpful, pleasant, kind. These people – they've been called 'emotional labourers' – are at risk from the phenomenon of *emotional burnout*.

A person who has 'burned out' is likely to suffer from apathy, cynicism and selfishness and will become unable to work effectively in any job that involves personal contact with the public. He or she can't maintain normal social relationships – divorce is common – and is emotionally fatigued and depressed.

Who is at risk?

The commercialisation of human feeling is one of the striking phenomena of our times. The 'emotional labourers' work primarily in the ever-expanding service sector, and although their work is often seen as relatively unskilled and undemanding, the level of stress-related disorders now experienced show that it can be in some ways as arduous as hard *physical* labour. These are some of the people we pay to be nice and helpful to us: air hostesses, receptionists, secretaries, waiters, nurses, librarians, teachers, PR consultants, radio and TV announcers, social workers and health service employees.

The symptoms of what we now call emotional burnout were first spotted a generation ago in a group of telephonists. More recently, waiters and waitresses in America have been found to be among the sufferers – relying heavily on tips for their income, their smile is their greatest asset. In the previous chapter we heard from two air hostesses how hard it can be, day in, day out to keep smiling.

The caring professions

Nurses, although having a generally high level of job satisfaction, suffer badly from emotional burnout. They tend to smoke and drink a lot. They leave the profession early. And they have a reduced life expectancy – four years below the average for working women. In fact, emotional burnout is a particular problem for those in the caring professions, who have unique sources of stress that come from the vital social roles they perform.

Before the Industrial Revolution changed the shape of the Western world, chronically ill people could be nursed at home, distressed people comforted by members of their extended family and tight-knit community, elderly people looked after by relatives and neighbours. Not of course that it was a Golden Age – many suffered alone and died needlessly. Nowadays we are able to provide vastly superior standards of care for people who find life hard, and as a society we are now so much richer in financial and human resources that we can afford to institutionalise these caring functions. The result is that the very people we now pay to carry out the vital caring tasks that we don't have the skill (or the time) to do adequately ourselves now tend to work within vast bureaucratic organisations.

They range from teachers to social workers and other social service employees; from public administrators to nurses, doctors and dentists; and they include a wide range of people dealing with the needy, sick, young and old – all those in need of a little help from society.

Studies of the caring professions have identified a number of areas of stress that can lead to disillusionment, emotional fatigue and eventual burnout:

* Working as part of a bureaucratic organisation (possibly state-run and vulnerable to cuts)
* Having no clear criteria of success
* Low status (and possibly low pay)
* Isolation
* Career plateaus
* Demanding clients

Bureaucracies

A caring professional must be something of an idealist. It's been argued that they need some illusion in their lives since it's only when they believe that there's hope in a situation that they can take effective action. However, the organisation they work for also has to look out for its own survival. It imposes demands on the staff which can lead to stressful conflicts.

The organisation needs:	The employee needs:
RULES to impose internal order	FREEDOM to act conscientiously
ADMINISTRATIVE TASKS to monitor and regulate itself	MORE TIME to spend with clients
A HIERARCHY of management (often including *uniforms*)	STATUS
RESTRICTIONS on what staff can do	SCOPE to work in any areas of perceived need

Paradoxically, working as part of a 'caring' organisation can often prevent workers from fulfilling the ideals that brought them to the organisation in the first place.

Looking at some of the state-run public service professions, we can see how the areas of stress we identified earlier are an almost inevitable part of the job. Hospital porters have low status and are at the bottom of a massive hierarchy; social workers, constantly required to 'put out' for demanding clients, with usually no clear, satisfying conclusion to their work, often have their problems exacerbated by a sense of isolation; teachers, again commonly required to give more than they receive, perhaps chafing against nit-picking bureaucracy, may reach plateaus relatively early in their careers.

A recent study of American teachers found that as many as one in four were vulnerable to burnout, while one in ten were already 'burned out' by the stress of their jobs. Many reported that they felt emotionally drained by teaching, and gave as their main sources of job dissatisfaction the lack of promotion opportunities, excessive paperwork and unsuccessful administrative meetings. Teachers said they felt that no matter how hard they worked they would not receive the recognition and appreciation that they needed.

This is not unique to America. A 1982 survey in the UK showed that teachers saw their work as very satisfying but highly pressured. More than half of the teachers would have liked more responsibility and, although self-esteem was high, many suffered from depression. Overall, the teachers didn't get the level of support they felt they needed to help them cope adequately with the demands of the job. They suffered from a variety of mental health problems.

Michael, a West Country teacher, had to leave his job after succumbing to emotional burnout.

The last day I actually attended my job was 11 October 1984. It hadn't been a particularly bad or unnecessarily stressful day [but] the experiences I went through that day were the last step in an accumulation of experiences that had gone on for some weeks, some months and probably for some years.

The day finished and I went home and my wife and I had one of those ... dispiriting evenings. I went out and got some Chinese food and we pushed it down ourselves, and then I felt too full and irritable, so I went to bed and went to sleep. I woke up ... pouring with sweat. I was in a very curious state of stress and anxiety, utterly motiveless about what I wanted to do the next day, whether I wanted to do it and how I'd do it when I got there.

My wife came up and took one look at me and said she'd seen me like that several times over the last few months and each time the degree of stress, frenzy about what I was doing and why I was there seemed to have mounted. She looked at me and I looked at her and we both said, 'For both of our sakes you must stop doing this, this is something you cannot go on doing to yourself.' I made the decision not to go back in the next day, that I would go and see a doctor and I would tell him what I had done.

What seemed to me a rather amazing thing was that I'd decided after twenty years of caring, responsible school teaching that that was it, and I wasn't going to go back to it.

Working with children, while rewarding, is emotionally very draining. Michael coped without trouble for many years, eventually rising to become head of an English department. He only began to suffer from burnout when he felt that the demands of the 'system' ran counter to the ideals of his job.

Society is now making enormous demands on teachers at exactly the same time when it is also, through the media, through the government, through Local Education Authorities, showing its lack of value of the teacher's role, its lack of respect for the teachers. And so teachers are trapped into working tremendously hard but for little approval, with little value given to their work. . . .

The tyranny of the organisation is something which grinds you down, it's a structure in which you are trapped. And no longer ever again do I want to carry out someone else's rules or decisions when fundamentally they seem to me against the interests of the children in front of me – children I like, children I work with.

Michael's is an almost classic case of emotional burnout. Sufferers describe themselves as lost in the gulf between their personal ideals and outside reality. It's usually the organisation they work for that's seen as the greatest source of this conflict because, as Michael bitterly points out, it should be providing them with the support to carry out their jobs effectively.

Social workers also face the problem of constantly 'giving' emotionally, but in their case it's often for little perceived result. Teamwork is a vital source of support. Someone who felt she was 'left out in the cold' is Northampton social worker Andy. Because of financial cutbacks the children's home where she worked was closed. She and her colleagues had the unpleasant task of disbanding the unit and transferring the children to other homes.

The way the staff coped with it was to be united, to support each other. We used to humour each other, to listen when we were feeling rough. It was very much a feeling of a team together, getting through a difficult time. And then suddenly, when that was finished, bang went the support system that was there as part of your everyday life.

Eventually she herself was transferred to a hostel for adolescent boys. Three staff worked a rota system to provide round-the-clock care for just one seventeen-year-old inmate. Without the emotional support she was used to, she just couldn't cope with the loneliness of the job.

I couldn't seek refuge in being busy. The place was run round the idea of the lads being independent, and so there was a distance you had to keep. There was a lady who cleaned the place, so you couldn't really flick a duster round. And so I would turn up at work at half past one . . . and I'd be there on my own until the same time the next day, whether or not the lad was there. You went to bed wondering whether he'd be knocking on the door during the night, whether he'd been out on the razzle and what sort of state he'd come back in. It was just uncertainty and waiting for a lot of the time.

I found I couldn't eat – I lost over a stone in a couple of months. I found it more difficult to make decisions. The thing that finally made me feel I had to seek help was the feeling of isolation. If you're keeping up with the herd you've got other people around you that you can turn to, not just to seek support from them but to be part of the team with them. You can face up to things that might otherwise be difficult.

It was draining all the energy I had – into getting nowhere at work. So there was precious little left. When I got home I just slept, and was irritable. I couldn't see a way out.

You could find support if you lifted the phone and said I'm finding things difficult, I need someone to talk to. But it isn't the same as going to work and having it as part of the basic tools of the trade that you worked with every day.

To get her over her immediate difficulties, Andy sought professional help. Salvation only came when the hostel was closed.

> I was moved to another children's home which was doing useful work and had a committed team. And within two days I was back to feeling fine. I wondered how I could have felt so dreadful such a short time before. It surprised me just how quickly it all just washed away. The acute distress from a week back had gone and I was back swimming in the stream again, being committed to a common task with colleagues who worked for the same end. I was accepted into the team and felt part of it. I believed in what I was doing again.

Status and self-esteem

Providing workers with a sense of *belonging* is vital, as Andy discovered. It gives access to the social support that we have already seen that colleagues can provide, and, moreover, gives a sense of status and purpose. Paul, a hospital porter in the Midlands, was caught between the emotional pressures of his job and its low status. He describes how one part of his role, putting patients at their ease, gave him a lot of satisfaction.

> One of the things that I found most enjoyable and most interesting was meeting new people every day. You're meeting people from all walks of life, all different ages, and it was really nice.
>   They've always got a smile and at the same time you've got a smile for them, although sometimes they really do not feel like smiling.

But, faced with personal problems, he began to find this aspect of his job difficult to cope with.

> When you've got to put on a happy face and all that every day, and things are going down the pan, then you really do not feel like it . . . things just get on top of you.

We had a new canteen open and one of the nursing officers was in there one day and she said, 'This is really nice
this place, what a shame we have to share it with the
porters and the ancillary staff.' And then you get those
who have trained – you've known them all the time, and
then when they're trained, they don't speak to you. I'll tell
you, it can really get to you. You treat people as friends,
you treat them as equals, and then all of a sudden it's no
longer like that. One minute they're all right with you, the
next they're not.

I was totally depressed and, at the same time, I had two
friends – one who committed suicide on Christmas Eve,
and another one who died shortly after New Year. I went for
the booze and the pills myself. You've got to be pretty far
down to do that. I didn't have any feelings at all. I was
completely numb, and I just didn't care, I'd just had
enough.

His union eventually spotted his problem, and referred him to
a stress counsellor. He is grateful for that, but believes it should
not have been the union's responsibility. 'What I'm saying is, in
a work situation, everybody should have the opportunity for
some kind of help, and it should be down to the management to
spot it.'

Although there are bound to be some conflicts between organisations and the caring individuals who work for them, there are
ways to minimise this and prevent burnout. Among the methods
that have been recognised are: giving workers a greater sense of
involvement by improving communications between colleagues
and perhaps letting them share in each other's work occasionally,
increasing their sense of effectiveness by letting them participate
in decision-making, providing social support, and allowing a
reasonable amount of time off for rest and recuperation from
their demanding clients.

Some of these are already incorporated to an extent into the
structure of the jobs of people at risk from burnout – but half
measures are not enough, as Michael, the teacher, found out.

One of the greatest pressures is never being able to escape
from the classroom and its work. People laugh. I have a lot

of friends who laugh at the teacher who with his six or seven weeks' summer holiday says, 'Look, I'm in a stressful job, I can't cope with it.' I have a close friend who suffered a very major crisis three or four years back, who once remarked very truly, 'The crunch point is when the six-week holiday is not long enough any more for the tensions to flow away, for the batteries to be recharged and for the enthusiasm to be there.'

Now that sounds very selfish, very demanding. What right have teachers to ask for that length of break from a job? Other people don't get that kind of break. But that is the kind of demoralisation of the resources that in many, many teachers the job imposes.

The Powys experience

In the rural Welsh county of Powys a unique combination of circumstances forced a major reorganisation of the health authority services about ten years ago. Until 1974, there was a complex bureaucracy running services that were split several ways. Hospital services were organised by boards and committees, community services were organised and paid for by local authorities, and GP services were run through executive councils.

For nurses in particular the situation was complicated further by yet another tier of management. Nurses working in hospitals were managed by nursing officers based in the hospital, while district nurses were organised by 'nurse managers' based in the community.

This complex system wasn't unique to Powys, but the problems it caused for nurses were greatly increased by the nature of the county. Communities are widely scattered, adding to the nurses' sense of isolation. Marion Morgan, now the Chief Administrative Nursing Officer for the county, recognises that the lack of communication between different sectors of the nursing service was damaging. 'Although in some places they talked to each other about patients, they didn't relate to each other in the way that we believed was necessary not only for good patient care, but for nurses themselves to feel an important and integral team.'

The result was that the nurses who were out on their own, doing community-based work, lost status both in their own eyes, the eyes of their colleagues, and – vitally – in the eyes of the patients for whom they cared.

> Nurses working in hospitals tended to be high status – seen as sort of 'high technology people', specialists in the drama of accidents and emergency work, specialists in intensive care and operating theatre and high surgical techniques.
>
> Nurses working in the community were seen by and large to be doing the more mundane day-to-day work, the boring work, the heavy work, the work with the elderly – which was perceived as perhaps not very exciting, not very interesting.

Reorganisation was clearly essential. The health authority realised that the differences in organisation across the county were affecting the nurses' job satisfaction and their ability to provide good patient care. To heal the splits, they went for an integrated approach. Nurses in any area – whether they were in a hospital or out in the community – would all be managed by one person who had a high degree of autonomy. Marion Morgan stresses that the changes had to be aimed at enhancing the nurses' status and making them feel more involved.

> They had all to be in the same uniform, whatever grade they occupied, whether they worked in the hospital or the community, so patients' perceptions of them as professionals were common irrespective of where they were working. They had to have access to the same sort of equipment. We couldn't have nurses working in hospital with all the benefits of sterile equipment, and nurses working in the home boiling equipment in fish kettles!

In 1974 all health services in the county were brought together into a single integrated organisation with a simplified management structure. According to Marion, the results were all that were hoped for.

> Now the nurses are able to call on the support of their peers within the hospital without feeling that calling on that

support demeans them in any way. Because their hospital colleagues have an understanding of the difficulties of looking after the chronically ill, and the terminally ill, at home, and because the *hospital* nurses come out into the *community*, they may well in fact have looked after those patients in hospital anyway. They've got an appreciation of these problems, and the work and the stress is therefore shared.

They get a great deal of mutual support based on a lot of mutual respect.

In Powys nursing is based firmly around teamwork, and power is devolved so that those lower down the hierarchy can feel that they can make more effective decisions. Pat is a matron now in sole control of eighty-three nursing staff and with regular contacts with many others. She has a large budget for nursing and supplies, over which she has a wide degree of discretion. This has increased her feelings of control and effectiveness. She can, to an extent, set her own criteria of success or failure.

I'm given a lot of flexibility in what I do with my own budget, and how I use it, and how I utilise members of staff. I don't have headquarters telling me 'you must do this'. I'm allowed to use my budget as I need to use it, as long as I stay within the constraints of that budget. I think that the flexibility of it means less stress because you can see where the needs are, and then can move the people around.

The improved communication within the organisation makes her feel more a part of a team – and helps the flow of information that's vital to the job.

For Gwen, one of the nurses working under Pat, job status and self-esteem have been enhanced. And from previously losing track of patients once they left her care she is now able to follow their progress – helping her to judge the success of the work she has done and to gain a feeling of reward and involvement. Her sense of isolation has also been removed. 'In the old system you more or less worked on your own. You were a district nurse and that was your lot. Your patient was admitted to the hospital and that was the end as far as you were concerned. Now, once your patient is admitted to the hospital you're encouraged to come in to visit and check on their progress.'

Because of the improved communications that are now a part of the matron's remit, the nurses are able to tackle their primary tasks more effectively and put their energies to better use. Marion Morgan admits that the system is not entirely without its problems, but the results are well worth while.

> There is a weakness in this system. The authority has to be prepared to invest more in training. It certainly has to accept the costs of staff meeting together on a regular basis. But having said that, those costs are more than outweighed by the improved communication, and certainly better staff morale – particularly a very much lowered incidence of sickness and absenteeism.

The lessons of Powys can be applied to any organisation that performs a caring function. The rules are simple. If you're in a profession where emotional burnout is a risk, it's worth asking what *your* organisation is doing to help. See how it comes out on the following checklist.

* Is there a minimum of inflexible hierarchy and a maximum of devolved decision making?
* Are people divided into small groups of professionals with related functions?
* Is there an emphasis on communication between people in different parts of the service?
* Is there quick and effective feedback of workers' difficulties for consultation and support?
* Have policy decisions been taken at the highest level to safeguard job status, pay and conditions of established workers?
* Are there resources allocated for retraining to keep abreast of developments in the profession and within the service?
* Is there flexibility of function – a chance to share and participate in others' work?
* Do workers have a way of getting pressure taken off them, to 'recharge their batteries'?

CHAPTER EIGHT

The stress of change

'Things ain't what they used to be', goes the old complaint. If you're talking about things at work it's quite true, they ain't, and that can be an important source of stress for the average working person. It's been found that even a change which improves the quality of life can be highly stressful, and unfortunately there are now major influences on employers which bring changes that are entirely detrimental to the work force.

We saw in Chapter One how homeostasis can help us to understand the reasons why any change can be stressful. Any living organism has to keep a balance with its surrounding environment, and if the environment changes, the organism must adapt to the new situation. The greater the change and the more complex the adaptation, the harder this is. It has been argued that organisms have only a limited capacity for tolerating stress, and if it's exceeded then the organism breaks down – the bough can only bend so far before it snaps.

Psychologist Barrie Hopson looks at change as a 'transition' in a person's life – a move from one state such as unemployment, youth or bachelorhood to another, such as employment, middle age or parenthood. He argues that in making this transition we undergo a complex cycle of reactions and feeling. He has identified seven stages in the process of adapting to change:

Immobilisation – being overwhelmed by the change and unable to cope.
Minimisation – trying to trivialise or even deny that the stressful change has happened.
Depression – as reality sinks in.
Letting go – accepting reality and starting to plan to cope.

Testing – starting coping, trying out new behaviour and new roles.
Search for meaning – trying to understand what has happened.
Internalisation – finally settling down to life after the change.

Of course, not everyone experiencing stressful change moves neatly from phase to phase of this cycle. If the change is desired, such as promotion, we may pass easily through the initial stages of shock and struggle or even miss them entirely and move straight on to the later stages where we begin to settle into our new role. Experience too will teach us a lot. But the cycle can be of value in helping to understand what has happened, to cope with shock or distress, to see a light at the end of the tunnel.

Roger had been dairy farming in mid-Wales for three years when the EEC changed the rules on him, and thousands like him, with the introduction of milk quotas. A stable, fulfilling work life suddenly became precarious. He felt a loss of control – he was no longer able to strike his own balance between his personal needs and the demands of the outside world. Unable to deal with this threat to his way of life he became traumatised.

> Money isn't everything in farming. Most people aren't in farming for the money, they're in there because it's a job which provides immense satisfaction – living in the countryside, working for yourself and reaping the benefits of your own hard work.
>
> Milk quotas came along [and] the only way I could come within the quota was to actually sell off the cows which I had just bought. It makes me feel very angry. I've worked hard to build this herd up – it's three or four years' work literally down the drain. In farming you have to plan five years ahead and the milk quotas were introduced on us literally in the space of a week. Nobody had any time to change or adapt to the situation . . . it's just stopped me in my tracks. We seem to have no control over our own destiny any more. We're just at the whim of the politicians now.
>
> As things stand at the moment I will never be allowed to reach my target production, which in effect means that I will never be able to make a living from my farm. I'm in a Catch-22 situation where I need to exceed my milk quota in

order to meet my commitments and make a living, but if I do so I face the probability of having to pay a penalty of 17.5 pence per litre produced in excess of quota – which is financial suicide when you consider that I'm only paid 14.5 pence per litre from the Milk Marketing Board!

The Milk Marketing Board set up a tribunal appeal system to which farmers could apply for a review of their individual circumstances. The denigration which I experienced at my tribunal hearing is something which I will never forget. We were treated like criminals. That evening I was totally depressed. I couldn't face milking my cows – my heart wasn't in it. The rug seemed to have been pulled out from under my feet. All the hard work and planning over the last four years had left me in a situation where in a good year I would only be able to meet my commitments. There would never be any opportunity for me to make even a basic living from my farm. There seemed no way of changing the situation. . . . The only avenue open to us is to try for a judicial review, but the likelihood of getting this seems quite remote.

I felt I'd completely lost control of the situation. I'd lost the motivation to carry on farming because I wasn't farming for myself, I was farming for the bank and the feed merchant and the fertiliser merchant. They were all making their profit, I was doing all the hard work and making no profit whatsoever and not going anywhere. It was very difficult to get up in the morning to go out and milk the cows. . . .

Roger's comments show how the initial shock of change, leading in his case to near-suicidal depression, is followed by adaptation. He was finally forced to accept that this change was virtually irresistible and he would have to accept it. Should he have chosen to fight on beyond any hope of victory, he would have faced the eventual exhaustion of all his personal resources, and the near certainty of physical or mental illness. His decision was to get out while the going was good.

The worst it got was standing on an underground station in London, waiting for a tube, and as the train pulled in a suicidal vision flashed across my mind. That was when I was at my lowest ebb, and after that I bucked up and I was determined to get up and fight. I didn't realise up until that time exactly the effect that the quotas were having on me mentally.

I don't think there's any future for me in farming – certainly not farming on borrowed money. If we had a small crisis that would effectively finish me, so looking at it objectively, the only thing for me to do is to try and sell the farm and look for some other occupation. I would miss farming. I have enjoyed it. I've enjoyed the independence, the freedom, the way of life, but there's no enjoyment in it now. The pressures are too much.

Since work holds such an important place in our lives, major changes at work can therefore pose major threats to our physical and mental stability. Some psychologists have attempted to draw up scales of the relative stressfulness of the various changes a person might have to cope with in their lifetime. For example, on Holmes and Rahe's Social Readjustment Rating Scale a change in your financial status – which is often work-related – would rank as being more stressful than the death of a close friend! If you think of the alteration in your lifestyle that would probably follow an increase in or loss of earning power, this makes sense.

On the same scale, changing your work hours or having trouble with your boss require about the same amount of adjustment as moving house. A change in work responsibilities comes out as only marginally less stressful than having a mortgage foreclosed, and retiring or losing one's job are about as momentous as marrying or having a reconciliation with an estranged spouse.

It's small wonder then, that changes in the way we work can wound us so deeply.

Roger's decision to accept the inevitable could be saving him from illness in the near future. It's believed by many psychologists that physical illness is an almost inescapable consequence of rapid and severe changes in one's way of life. The following life stress ranking based on the 'Social Readjustment

Scale,' is used by psychologists and stress counsellors to help provide an early warning of possible stress-related ill health. It can only give a fairly rough indication of the stress people are under and help them to make an educated guess as to how severe its effects may be, because it cannot take into account the sort of person they are (some people are far better at coping with the slings and arrows of life than others).

The death of a spouse is given an arbitrary value of 100 Life Change Units (LCUs) and other sources of stress are measured in relation to this. To assess stress subjects, add up the number of LCUs they've incurred during the last year.

It is claimed that a score of more than 150 'incurred' – in any one year is associated with at least a 50–50 chance of a major health breakdown the following year. (From R. H. Rahe, 1969, in *Psychotropic Drug Response – Advances in Prediction* (Editors P. R. A. May and J. R. Wittenborn, Illinois)).

Family	
Death of spouse	100
Divorce	73
Marital separation	65
Death of close family member	63
Marriage	50
Marital reconciliation	45
Major change in health of family member	44
Pregnancy	40
Gaining new family member	39
Major change in number of arguments with spouse	35
Child leaving home	29
Troubles with in-laws	29
Spouse starting or ending work	26
Major change in number of family get-togethers	15
Personal	
Jail sentence	63
Major injury or illness	53
Sexual difficulties	39
Death of close friend	37
Outstanding personal achievement	28
Major change in living conditions	25
Major revision of personal habits	24
Moving house	20
Major change in recreation	19

Major change in social activities	18
Major change in sleeping habits	16
Major change in eating habits	15
Vacation	13
Christmas	12
Minor violation of the law (e.g. traffic offence)	11

Work

Being fired	47
Retirement	45
Major business adjustment	39
Changing to new line of work	36
Major change in responsibilities	29
Trouble with boss	23
Major change in working conditions	20

Financial

Major change in financial state	38
Large mortgage or loan (e.g. house purchase)	31
Mortgage foreclosure	30
Small mortgage or loan (e.g. car or TV purchase)	17

Psychologist John Nicholson has developed a modified version of the Holmes and Rahe 'Life Events' questionnaire which helps you to determine how *you* react to major stressful events.

Here is a list of the 10 most stressful life-events. Put a tick in one or other of the two boxes beside each item to indicate whether or not you have had first-hand experience of it during *the last* year.

		Yes	No
1	Retirement	☐	☐
2	Being fired from your job	☐	☐
3	Serious personal injury or illness	☐	☐
4	Marital reconciliation (after being separated)	☐	☐
5	Pregnancy	☐	☐
6	Marital separation	☐	☐
7	Marriage	☐	☐
8	Divorce	☐	☐
9	Imprisonment	☐	☐
10	Death of husband (or wife)	☐	☐

Although not all these events sound unpleasant, they are all stressors (remember that all change is, by definition, stressful). To work out how stressful your life has been, for each Yes answer you have given, take stress points to the value of the question number, i.e. one stress point for a Yes to Question 1, two stress points for Question 2, and so on. The higher your score, the more stressful your life has been recently.

If you have more than 20 points, you have had more than your share of misfortunes. But not everyone who falls into this category will necessarily be suffering from the effects of stress. So much depends on how you react to major problems. This too can be measured. If you want to discover how much *impact* a particular stressful event has had on you, keep your stress scores and read through the following statements, indicating in one of the boxes besides each one how frequently it has applied to you and the event in question, during the last week.

		Not at all	Rarely	Some- times	Often
1	I thought about it when I didn't mean to	☐	☐	☐	☐
2	I avoided letting myself become upset when I thought about it	☐	☐	☐	☐
3	I tried to forget about it	☐	☐	☐	☐
4	I had trouble falling asleep or staying asleep, because of pictures or thoughts about it that came into my mind	☐	☐	☐	☐

Score 0 for every 'Not at all' answer, 1 for 'Rarely', 2 for 'Sometimes' and 3 for an 'Often' answer. If you have a score of more than 6 for any of the life-events you identified in the previous section, then you should double your score of stress points for that particular item.

Recalculate your stress score so far, bearing in mind that any score over 20 indicates that your life has been on the stressful side recently. Then proceed to the next stress factor.

(From *Fitness* magazine, August 1985)

Is work good for you?

What makes the post-war era so precarious for the working man or woman is the sheer pace of the changes being forced on us. It's partly the effect of new technology and foreign competition, which put jobs directly under threat, but it's partly too an effect of social change – most notably in the status and aspirations of women.

Employment, despite all the sources of stress we've already found, is on the whole good for you. Apart from the obvious function of providing us with the money to live, it has important psychological functions – supplying many of the things we need for our mental as well as our purely physical well-being.

It's been said that work is a person's strongest link with reality. It gives us a sense of meaning and purpose by providing structure to our lives, a chance to share our experiences with others, a source of personal status and identity, a set of goals to achieve and activities to perform. These benefits tend to outweigh the stresses of work. By and large people would rather be in work than out of it.

When British Steel ended steelmaking in the strip mills at Corby in 1981, Jerry had a secure job in BSC's tube works. Although on the same site as the steel plant, the tube works were at that time largely unaffected by the massive redundancies that hit the town. But Jerry could feel the winds of change blowing. To him, job security was the most important thing to have, so he made the seemingly paradoxical decision to quit his job in the tube works, eventually finding a similar job to his old one but in a company which he felt had a more secure future.

I was pretty secure because I worked in the tube works, but there were a lot of rumours that the tube works wouldn't last much longer because the steel strip came from the steel side, and consequently it would no longer function as a profitable unit. I decided that steel-working probably would completely cease in Corby so I decided to try other ventures.

I went to a local company selling cars and trucks. That was OK for a while but the money started drying up in Corby and obviously there was no money to sell or buy cars or trucks. So therefore I wasn't making money there.

I was looking for something that would give me security, but the companies that were coming to Corby at first were very small, employing two or three people, six people, a dozen people – high-tech companies but the sort that didn't want the labour force, the unskilled type of labour that Corby has got. I was waiting for a company that would come along and offer me a secure future.

In the tube works I was an inspector. RS Components were advertising for inspectors so I applied for a job and I was successful in the interview. RS Components is a completely different ball game to the ventures we've all known in the past in Corby. . . . One of the things I like about the place is that everybody uses the canteen here – the directors use it, the managers use it, everybody uses it. We've a free bus service, which we never had at BSC, and we work under very clean conditions. But most of all I find that I feel secure – that's the key to this place.

Why work at all?

One of the effects of the changing nature of work, growing unemployment and increased leisure time is an erosion of our traditional idea of the value of work – the so-called 'protestant work ethic'. There is an increasing acceptance of the idea that personal fulfilment and work don't have to go hand in hand.

Jim is a case in point. After years working as a road-mender in Corby, he was suffering from ill health and also wanting more free time to care for his handicapped son. The council's offer of voluntary redundancy gave him the chance to turn his back on a job that had become almost entirely negative in its effects, and to reconstruct his life.

I accepted voluntary redundancy because I had problems with my back and I also was allergic to sunlight, so it made sense to get out. We had a mentally handicapped son and he needed a lot of looking after. There's no way I could have worked and given him the love and support that he needed.

In the early days when I was unemployed, like probably everybody else I felt guilty. I decided that I would try and make the best of it, so I've got myself involved in a handicapped group, and I do as many jobs in the house as I can to keep myself busy, and I try not to feel guilty – because there's enough people unemployed along with me. I do feel stress at times but I try to put it out of my mind.

I did find that there was a pattern which came about, and I was getting stress-related illnesses. Nothing bad, but my wife discovered that when any big decision or work in the house came up I used to get symptoms like flu. It was always related to something that was coming up. I think it was perhaps a lack of confidence because I was unemployed, but when you realise what's causing it, it's far easier to throw it off.

Jim faced change at its worst, with a severely reduced income and consequently a restricted lifestyle, changes in his pattern of daily activities and removal of his goals. After the initial period of shock as this sank home, he was able to correct all of these problems with the exception of income. What makes his *un*-employment better than his previous employment is that he's also been able to improve his scope for decision-making and to develop new skills – in fact to *increase* his control over his daily life.

I feel quite happy about the situation now. My wife's quite happy having me at home. We probably do more together. We have days out with the handicapped kids and apart from money I've got no depressing worries about anything. I go to the welfare rights advice centre in Corby, and I feel that between the centre and the handicapped group I get more or less the same type of camaraderie that I used to get at work, plus I've got the allotment and they're a good bunch of lads down there. If someone was to tell me I'd never be employed again for the rest of my life I don't think I would worry.

New skills for old

A lot of the satisfaction of work comes from developing and using skills. Nowadays, new skills are needed to cope with new ways of working, and old skills often become obsolete. We don't have to look much further than the troubles on Fleet Street to see how strongly skilled workers react to the idea of obsolescence. If changes are truly necessary for the well-being of a company, then the workers won't in the end be able to avoid them – although in many cases that means redundancy. The other side of the coin is that managers all too often fail to realise the severity of the threat the changing nature of work poses to the people on the sharp end. If Holmes and Rahe are right, being thrown onto the scrap heap is almost as big a blow as being severely injured, and certainly more stressful than merely losing some of your earning power.

The trouble is that management tend to take on new technology in order to increase their control over production, rather than necessarily to increase production itself. Glasgow psychologists David Buchanan and David Boddy found this led to problems in a biscuit-making factory when microprocessors were introduced on one production line. The skilled 'ovensmen' found that their job satisfaction was increased by operating the computer-controlled machinery, while the 'doughmen' found life much worse.

The reason was that the equipment enhanced some skills (giving the men who ran the ovens more control, interest and challenge), whilst replacing other skills (reducing the men who mixed the dough to mere servants of the machinery). If management had had different objectives, the investigators thought, rather than pursuing the aim of reducing operator involvement to a bare minimum they might have reorganised the work in order to give the doughmen more control and involvement.

Recent research has found that, contrary to popular myth, most union members *don't* object in principle to the introduction of new technology. Many even request it, seeing it as a means of safeguarding their jobs by making the company they work for more competitive, and of enhancing their job satisfaction by improving their skills and giving them more control over the work they do. The real blame for the ineffectualness of Britain's move to new technology is laid at the door of management.

Fishy chips

Many researchers argue that unless the introduction of new technology is carefully controlled, the effect is to give a limited number of staff more skills while cutting down on the skills required of the majority. The temptation for management is to form an elite of skilled 'technocrats' to control production whilst de-skilling most of the shop floor. Women workers, traditionally badly paid, are often used to carry out the de-skilled tasks.

Dave, a foreman at an electronics factory, has seen this trend develop since the days when he started on the production line, wiring electronic components and electrical transformers on to printed circuit boards.

When I was actually doing the work, large quantities would be twenty to thirty boards, but now an average quantity would perhaps be five or six thousand boards a week going through here, and that is one of the greatest changes. The work has got that much smaller as well. The transformers are very, very small now. They used to be large things – you used to push them around on wheels in some instances! Plus there's very little wiring as such – we used to get the wires on reels and make our own wiring looms, now it's all on the printed boards, the circuit is etched.

The manual work is getting less and less – the machines are doing it. What is being done is getting more and more mundane. The person's just putting components on the board and one of my problems is keeping them happy, keeping them interested in their work. When I first became a supervisor they were doing skilled jobs assembling the complete units, whereas now a printed board just plugs into the completed unit. We've got all the aids for the operators to do the job and so they become bored. And my job's changed in that you have to have a laugh and a joke with them, keep them happy. It helps, it breaks their day.

As the manual tasks have got more and more de-skilled, the technical tasks have got more and more skilled. The education level is increasing among the people that are coming into the factory now – I know of quite a few of them that have got a degree. And they're not really on the shop floor as such, they're divorced from it. They'll write the test program and that's passed on to the shop floor and put into the machine and the machine does the testing. Obviously someone presses the button for the machine to work.

A lot of the boring jobs will disappear. The operators are being found other work, their jobs are changing. Maria, her job changed. She's come off the bench, she's now writing programs for the machines. A lot of jobs will be phased out, shall we say. It will be automated – in America you'll find they have machines to move the boards. A machine can be automatically reloaded and downloaded and the boards can be moved along to the next stage. That's what's going to happen to the boring tasks, the robots are going to do them.

Maria, who Dave sees as an example of the new breed of skilled workers, has found that the introduction of new process equipment has greatly improved her working life.

> I used to work on one of the machines which inserts the components into the boards. I went then on to repairing printed boards and then on to production engineering, where I now write the programs for the printed boards.
>
> It's very interesting. You learn new things every day – you're not doing the same thing. You do the whole thing yourself – you write the whole program yourself. It's very boring just putting the components on the board – that's all you do all day ... I enjoy the work very much. What I want to do in the future is write programs for different machines and make a career out of it.

But for most of the production-line workers, job satisfaction has decreased. Their task now is essentially just to insert electronic components which are selected by a machine into a circuit board at a spot indicated by the machine. And the machine then does all the rest. Paul, a production-line worker, feels this simplified task provides him with no reward other than a pay packet at the end of the week.

> Oh, I just put them in there and wait for them to come out the other end, which is, you know, extremely boring and monotonous ... sort of standing about all day, putting them in like a moron. If you can get a job where you're rebuilding a whole board then it's not too bad. But the usual jobs are the sort of moronic things you can train a maggot to do. And they're just – well, boring. It's not really worth coming here just to fit things in like that all day long, it's just terrible.

A well run organisation will devote time and resources to

planning for the effects of necessary change. The anxiety and apprehension raised in the work force, the adjustments that they'll need to make, and the extra effort that will involve, are bound to cause stress to the workers and problems for the management. Anticipation is the key.

Buchanan and Boddy have come to the conclusion that introducing new technology into the workplace needn't be a threat to the workers, provided that the management who bring it in accept a responsibility to consider the social and psychological consequences. They've studied companies where the work force have accepted or even welcomed new technology and have found three important factors:

* Employment policies that emphasise retraining and transfer and the avoidance of forced redundancy.
* The perception that new technology can do a job better.
* Where change happens frequently it's regarded as normal and is anticipated.

They believe that the effect of these factors, all of which can be controlled by management, is to remove the sense of threat from technological change. In none of the companies studied which paid attention to these factors were there any redundancies through the introduction of new technology, nor were there any serious industrial relations problems because of it.

These are the guidelines *your* management should be following. Are they?

* Don't change everything at once. Bring in changes a little at a time.
* Leave work teams together if they're working well.
* Make sure there's adequate feedback about new methods.
* Allow adequate time for people to learn new ways.
* Give your staff real involvement – listen to them, plan ahead with them, be frank with them.
* Look specifically at ways of reducing stress – job fit, control and responsibility, work load, relationships, participation.

(Adapted from 'Managing Stress in Organisational Change', Dept. of Employment Work Research Unit, May 1984.)

Making progress

Career development is a source of worry to many professional people, especially those in management to whom careers can assume overriding importance, and the things that stress people change as their position changes. A step forward in a career brings higher status and greater rewards, but more challenges, while a stagnating career may be undemanding but brings fears of redundancy or obsolescence, frustration or loss of status. Career plateaus are a commonly reported source of job dissatisfaction for management employees.

Although career progression entails change, it's a change that is usually under control and for which the necessary coping skills can be developed. And it's a change that brings rewards and can often remove sources of frustration. But with today's emphasis on youth and dynamism, older staff may find it increasingly hard to progress in their careers. There's sound evidence that the mid-life crisis that's found its way into the language as the 'male menopause' really exists. A survey in 1982 by UMIST found that between the ages of 40 and 49 there's a mid-career crisis that leads to a slow decline in satisfaction with most aspects of work.

Cary Cooper has pointed out that under such circumstances, at a time in their lives when many workers are seeking more stability, the only way for them to progress may be through a major change of career direction with all of its consequent uncertainties. He warns that 'unless managers adapt their expectations to suit new circumstances, "career development stress", especially in later life, is likely to become an increasingly common experience'.

Coping with change

It is possible to provide yourself with a set of personal skills that will help you to cope with any changes that working life forces upon you.

The essential element is to learn to look within yourself and ask honest questions about how you feel about the new situation you're in. Barrie Hopson has drawn up the following list of pointers:

Know yourself, your feelings and attitudes. What do you stand
to gain or lose? How can you help yourself to cope?

Know your new situation – what does it involve? How should
you behave? Can you try aspects of it out in advance?

Know other people who can help by providing you with a sense of
your own worth, someone to talk to, information, a perspective on your troubles.

Learn from the past. How did this happen? Has anything like it
happened before? If so, how did you (or others) cope?

Look after yourself. You're the most important person you
know, so keep fit, eat sensibly, talk positively to yourself.

Let go of the past. What's done is done – don't brood. Vent your
anger constructively.

Set goals and make action plans. Decide what's best for you and
work out how to do it. Think of alternatives.

Look for the gains you've made. Think positively. What have you
gained or learned? What new opportunities have emerged?

In the final chapter in the book we'll be looking in some detail
at some of the ways in which you can put these recommendations
to best effect, with tips on diet, relaxation, assertiveness and
how to set and attain your personal goals.

CHAPTER NINE

The working woman

The last twenty years have brought the biggest change in the role of women at work since the Industrial Revolution. In 1961, the proportion of British women who were working or looking for work was 41 per cent. By the census of 1981 the figures had been almost reversed, with 57.7 per cent of women now working or unemployed and only 42.3 per cent not seeking work. The changeover came midway between those dates – since 1971 the non-working woman has been in the minority.

Women are still concentrated in the low-paid industries, and indeed number the great majority of the low paid. They constitute the majority of part-time workers and home-workers. But the further emancipation of women, with more equal opportunities at work and anti-discrimination laws, has led to an increase in the number of working women with good qualifications and a desire to progress further in their chosen careers and gain greater job satisfaction.

But now other challenges are rearing their heads, and they're not ones that can be tackled by laws. Women are finding that new opportunities at work bring new stresses – often quite unexpected ones. In this chapter we'll be looking at some of these sources of stress and seeing how working women have tackled them.

The problems start when a woman steps outside her 'traditional' role, which is in many ways a subservient one. Rosemary, who runs a financial consultancy service, discovered that getting to the top in her career was only half the fight. Not only did she have all the stresses that any man in her position might expect to face, she had the double difficulty of being a *woman* in that job.

There are problems dealing with consultants on a day-to-day basis, when you are in a position of authority over people who would naturally assume in this industry that the person managing them would be a man, especially when you're talking about men of, say, fifty, who do not take kindly to being told off by a woman. It's happened sometimes where I've been in a situation of conflict with someone, which is a perfectly normal situation which would have to be handled by a man manager ... and I hear later on the grapevine that he thinks I'm a man-hater. You see, whereas they'll take it like a man from a man, they won't necessarily take it like a man from a woman.

They don't like the fact that I'm not an old bag, because they could handle that a bit better. You can see it on their faces sometimes – they walk in, they take one look at me and they go 'Oh, how am I going to handle this one?' So then they have to adjust, and you can see they're thinking about how they mustn't put a foot wrong – perhaps she's a militant feminist!

I was at a meeting a couple of weeks ago with a couple of very high-powered people – a technical director and a marketing director of a big company. I was in a position where I wanted to sell them something. We were getting on terrifically well. We'd had a good lunch. Then I started to talk about the things that we could do ... and then the crunch came as it invariably does when I'm not in a position of authority but I am the one who has to ask for something. It was treated as a joke of course: 'That's great. Well, what we must do is find two hours to sit down and discuss this over lunch. Or better still, dinner. How about that, Rosemary?'

The worst part of it is that you have to smile. You can't actually get up and clump someone round the face and say 'Do me a favour, get lost!' You have to smile and take it in a good-humoured manner and then go back to the office and smash a wall. And I'm not talking about guys of fifty or sixty. I'm surprised how young they were – we're talking about mid-thirties, who ought to know better.

Entrenched attitudes

Rosemary's discovery that she faces increased stress because she's a woman in the job is one which is familiar to most career women. It's quite clear that one of the major sources of stress for a modern career woman, in fact probably her single largest source of stress, is the attitude of other people – both men and women.

Nobody likes unpleasant surprises. We want to know how to expect the people around us to behave, and so we try to make them fit our stereotyped ideas of how they *should* behave. We all do it – it's a mental trick which makes it easier to survive in a crowded, bustling world. Unfortunately for the modern woman, most people still have a traditional stereotype for her to conform to, and when she doesn't it upsets their preconceptions and is likely to be seen as a threat.

This conversation was recently overheard on a London commuter train:

> *First businessman:* 'Oh, I've got nothing against women working. I've half a dozen men working for me and one woman, and she's as good as any of them. Mind you . . . she tends to get a bit shrill and strident when she can't get her own way.'
>
> *Second businessman:* 'A bit of a nag, eh?'
>
> *First businessman:* 'That's right. Aren't they all occasionally? I just have to tell her who's boss.'

That astonishing exchange makes the point nicely. The woman in question is quite possibly no more aggressive or outspoken when she 'can't get her own way' than any of her male colleagues. But that sort of behaviour is expected of them and not of her. Her boss, who would no doubt approvingly describe the men in the office as 'go-getting', dismisses her as strident, shrill and a nag. And, although he must often have to show his staff 'who's boss', he feels so threatened by the woman in particular that he makes a point of telling his travelling companion that he's asserted his authority over her. He's looking for some kind of reassurance. In other words, this man is behaving in a way which must be an unnecessary source of stress to his female subordinate simply because her very presence in her job is a stress to him!

Rosemary says she feels stressed a lot of the time.

> When an inspector faces you with some really inane comment about women, you actually sense anger writhing inside, and you feel if [you'd] met him in the street [you'd] punch him on the nose. But I'm behind a desk and I have to be polite, so you calm yourself down. It happens all the time but you learn to live with it. I've found that for me the best way of coping with it is humour. It's sometimes the only way I get through a day sane. Otherwise I would go home with that anger, and going home with that anger is dreadful. I've got two children at home who rely on me being wonderful.

Role conflict

All too often, however, women can be their own worst enemies. The pressure to conform to traditional female behaviour patterns doesn't come solely from men. The modern career woman is probably educated to a higher level than her older female relatives and unlike them is trying to find satisfaction in work outside the home. Mothers, aunts, grannies, older sisters may all have wished her to succeed at college and at work, but when they see the reality of it they can easily come to interpret her hard-won independence as an implied attack on their own way of living. So they go on to the attack themselves, questioning her behaviour, her standards, her lifestyle – and of course wondering out loud when she's going to 'settle down' and start a family.

Some of these arrows find their mark, and the career woman ends up questioning her aims in life. By the time she's in her late thirties she knows she must have faced up to at least one crucial question: work or family? It often seems to be a straight choice between one or the other, as Margaret found. She had a responsible position at the National Westminster Bank, and a good career ahead of her. Having a family hadn't at first seemed an important career consideration. Then one day . . .

> I suddenly realised that here I was, I was approaching thirty.

It's a watershed, you know. I'd always expected to have a
family, but I'd been working since I was sixteen, and I was
enjoying my job very much. I'd done some interesting
things. Well, was I now going to have a family?

[By the time] I was approaching my mid-thirties . . . I did
want a family. I'd been working for nearly twenty years. I
thought, I'm loth to give all this up, but I don't want to
give up having a baby. How am I going to actually put all
these things together? What happens at forty when I wake
up and I don't have a child? I've got a superb career which
I've enjoyed, but something's missing here as well. So it was
a very, very difficult decision to make.

Most working women are mothers, and most mothers work.
The first of the new skills that a would-be career woman has to
learn is therefore how to carry out the tricky balancing act
between career and family. Planning either is not particularly
hard – and there are plenty of people to give advice. But planning
for *both* a career and a family?

The trouble is that the social changes of the last couple of
decades have happened too fast for organisations and individuals
to cope. Little has been done to tackle the particular problems
of women's increasing desire to have both a planned career and
a family. One exception, however, is the National Westminster
Bank. They've recognised that women are a pool of potential
management talent that they would be unwise to ignore, and
have brought in a scheme to help women pick up their careers
where they left off to have a family. Provided they put in a
minimum two weeks' work a year, they can have up to five
years away from their jobs to raise a family. Anne, who adminis-
ters the career break scheme, believes it to be an effective answer
to a variety of problems.

In the seventies we [realised] that women weren't coming
through to management in anything like the number we'd
expected. . . . We'd put a lot of money into training these
people and they were very valuable to us, and we are always,
in an organisation like ours, short of management talent.

We decided that the best way of approaching it was to allow the women a career break of up to five years, but during that time we'd ask them to come back and work [a minimum of] two weeks every year. . . . The other thing we needed to do was to keep them in touch during the year, so I send out a monthly pack to each of the women in which I write a letter about new developments and send them things like our house magazine, and we have one annual seminar each year so all the women come together to meet each other and see how they're going on. . . .

It's not designed particularly for women who have reached management – it's for women with managerial potential. Most of the women on the scheme are still in the clerical grades.

Since the women on this scheme are encouraged to do some work while their children are growing up, but are not under pressure to do more than the minimum two weeks a year, it has the effect of breaking down the hard-and-fast distinction between work and family. The women are not under quite so much pressure to conform to either of the two restricting stereotypes – career woman or housewife. Margaret found this was the way out of her quandary.

I couldn't say whether or not I would ever have come back at the end of my maternity leave. It's too difficult a decision to take when you're working. It's quite easy to say: I'm going to miss this stimulus too much. You don't know what it's like to be at home with a baby. You don't know how you're going to feel at the end of that time. You also don't know the emotional effect that a child is going to have on you, the pull that you're going to feel as a mother.

The option was open to me to have an extended maternity leave, if you like, and it has to be said that that had a bearing on the fact that I was going to have a baby. I wanted to have the best of both worlds and I was lucky to be in a profession that allowed me to do that.

It is important that you are seen to be putting in your commitment, as well as the bank putting in theirs. You can't do that without wondering: Have I made adequate arrangements? What happens if the child is ill? It's the thousand and one things that you have to try and think of to receive job satisfaction for yourself and also make sure that your family doesn't suffer in any way.

It's a problem for women – we do want to be all things to all people. You don't want to feel that you're less of a mother or you're less of an employee by combining home, family and career.

Making your own opportunities

More and more women are demanding this kind of consideration from their employers. When they can't find it, they're forced either to abandon having a family, or to abandon or postpone career plans and just take whatever work they can get that enables them to meet family commitments. Four and a half million women work as part-timers or home-workers, and very few could claim that it was any kind of career.

A lucky few have been able to create their own balance between their careers and home lives. New technology can be invaluable in this respect – with computers you can bring your office into your own home. Over the next few years we'll be seeing a boom in the number of people, especially women, working from home with the aid of new technology and pursuing careers in journalism, advertising, accountancy, insurance, finance, planning, law – the list is endless.

F International is a computer consultancy that's tapping this potential. Most of its employees are women computing specialists, and many work from home. Janice is one woman who's found this an ideal solution to her 'balancing act'.

I started working in the computer industry fourteen years ago for ICL. After about seven years I had my daughter. I wasn't sure that I actually wanted to go back to work full-time after that, but I felt that I didn't actually want to stay at home all of the time. So I joined F International on their technical panel as a freelance programmer, and did several years programming and analysis and moved on to project management. Last year I decided I'd like to try doing a sales role, so I took a part-time salary to do that job, and eventually, I imagine, I will go back to work full time as my daughter gets older.

On a typical day I'll take my daughter to school and then either go off to visit a client or go back home again and catch up on my paperwork. I make most of my own appointments and therefore I can make them to suit my own routine, which means that normally I would arrange them during the school hours so that I'm there to take her to school in the morning and collect her in the evening. Obviously that doesn't always work, but most of the time I can do that and I can do the paperwork at other times to suit myself, so I'm around most of the time for her.

There are some disadvantages. I don't get away from the job. It's always there, sitting in the study waiting for me. The post arrives, even on days when I'm not working. But apart from that, it fits in very well.

The best thing about the job is that I can progress my career at this level. Not just earn money but actually have a career and progress through F International whilst still being able to work part time.

'Woman's work'

Although there's been little research into the different responses to stress of men and women, the facts that are beginning to emerge support feminist contentions that there's no inherent difference between the sexes.

A study of Post Office workers has found that women suffer more from stress-related illnesses than men do, but other researchers point out that women tend to be under more stress anyway because of the dual role they try to perform. A report on stress at work by the European Foundation for the Improvement of Living and Working Conditions states that 'most working women are working wives who do as much work in the home "after hours" as they do in the workplace'.

It's been estimated that a working housewife puts in a 12- or 13-hour working day when time spent at the job is added to time spent doing housework. The European Foundation report suggests that this is one of the reasons why women will accept unfavourable working conditions or low pay provided the work is only a short travel time from home, gives them usable lunch breaks (for shopping or a return home) and gives adequate time off at the weekend or in the form of holidays to enable them to meet family commitments.

Having found the freedom to work, whether it's by abandoning the idea of having a family or by taking a low-paid job near home, or by recourse to a daily waltz to crêche or childminder, the working woman will probably do her nine to five in an office or factory that segregates her from the men. Women are concentrated in a few categories of occupation, and generally at a lower level. They escape from the kitchen sink only to be given 'woman's work' by their bosses.

A third of clerical workers are women but only a seventh of professional people are. A survey in 1980 showed that nearly two-thirds of women worked only with other women. The result is that they come to see their jobs as being low status – work that men can't do or more probably wouldn't wish to do. There is a tremendous sexual division of labour that's a mirror of the division found in the home. And because of the difficulty of getting to work in the first place, and the subordination of women who do work, pay levels are substantially lower. Only one in six women earn more than their husbands or work longer hours. The man's role as primary breadwinner is thus reinforced.

Dual career families

Perhaps the best answer to the clash that most women find between home and work lies in the so-called dual career family. Since time immemorial housewives have worked to earn a supplementary wage, but in the dual career household the female partner's incentive for working is not principally financial – it's for her own self-satisfaction. The career woman rightly demands that her work be treated as equally important as the man's.

The danger is that dual career couples will be thrown into competition with each other. Few of us have the skills to cope with the conflicts of interest that are bound to arise.

First of all there's that thorny old problem of role conflict to be overcome. It's not reasonable for the career man to expect the career woman to do all his washing and ironing for him, and to take the major part in rearing the family. A division of labour along non-traditional lines is needed, but first the couple have to throw out their preconceived ideas of male and female roles within the family.

Then there are problems which arise when career decisions have to be made. Perhaps one partner would face a setback in their career if the other were to seize a promotion opportunity that meant moving to a different part of the country. Only by working closely together in a trusting relationship can a flare-up be prevented.

Dual career couples tend to be socially isolated. Neither has as much free time as they would like because of their increased responsibilities to partner and children. The inevitable spill-over between their work and home lives can lead to social dilemmas. In short, neither is any longer a free agent.

Some psychologists have tried to define precisely the types of person who can have a successful dual career relationship. They identify four or more different categories of personality into which each partner could fall, based on factors such as assertiveness, involvement or caring, and can thus come up with at least sixteen possible combinations.

Janet Macdonald, who argues for a pragmatic approach to relationships in her book *Climbing the Ladder: How to be a Woman Manager*, observes:

> Thinking about all my married friends, many of whom run dual career marriages, the combination that seems to work best is that of temperamental opposites. One tends to be phlegmatic, the other volatile and short-fused. The latter goes off like a bottle of pop after a good shaking, and the former administers a pat on the shoulder and says, 'There, there, darling, never mind. Calm down.' It tends, in my experience, to be the wife who fizzes, but it is not always that way.

Coping with a dual career relationship

* Discuss what you'd like from your work and home lives. Understand the effects your needs have on your partner's freedom of action.
* Try to limit your needs so you both have some degree of freedom and an opportunity to cope.
* Make long-term plans to keep work/home conflicts to a minimum.
* Compartmentalise your work and home lives – again reducing conflicts.
* Make flexible career plans around yourself rather than any organisation – be prepared to move, change, retrain.

Taking it like a man

The strategy that many women adopt when they see how the odds are stacked against them by the male-influenced organisation of work is to become 'one of the boys'. If you want to be accepted in a man's world, then why not behave like a man? Just as the men apply stereotypes of female behaviour to the women they work with – with the consequences we've already seen – so women all too often make the same mistake and come to believe that their stereotyped idea of the successful career man's behaviour is really the best way to get on in the job. The results can be disastrous.

Recent studies indicate that heart attacks among women executives may be on the increase. It's a medical myth that women just don't get heart attacks – anyone can have a coronary if they do the wrong thing. What's happening now is that women are putting themselves at risk by adopting coronary-prone behaviour patterns.

Coronary heart disease still affects twice as many men as women. The doctors usually say that a woman's hormones somehow protect her, but there's no clear evidence that this is so. It obscures the point that women are just as prone to stress-related illnesses as men, but they tend to have *different* illnesses. A working man may give himself a heart attack while his stay-at-home wife, bored and lonely, falls prey to agoraphobia which could lead to a lifelong dependency on tranquillisers. But what, instead, if that wife was working in a similar job to her husband, and behaving in a similarly aggressive, competitive way? It now looks as if she too would be a coronary candidate. It's been proved that although Type A women suffer less heart disease than Type A men, they suffer more heart disease than Type Bs, male or female. And there's not a lot of difference in the heart attack rates between Type B men and women.

There are also many occasions when behaviour which would be perfectly normal in a man is not accepted from a woman, no matter who she is. Rosemary found this out, to her annoyance:

> We had a change of inspector ... which was a shame. ... The new manager came in to try and persuade me that what we really wanted to do was to be with their new inspector, and I tried to tell him that I really didn't want to. The upshot was that the new manager went above my head, to my managing director, on the grounds that he thought he ought to speak to him about why we wouldn't change over because he felt that there may be more to it than just the fact that we were happy with this inspector – the implication being that there was some kind of intimate relationship going on.
>
> The guy could not accept that there was a perfectly logical reason to keep continuity going with a man from a company. There had to be something else. Now, he would never have thought that if I were a man.

So how should a woman behave in a stressful encounter if she's not to be browbeaten? Janet Macdonald believes that a key factor is the insecurity that many men feel when they're in a confrontation with a woman. The answer is for the woman to stand her ground.

> What it all boils down to is refusing to be pressurised just because the other party is a man. The more they try, the more you refuse to give way and continue to state your case. Constant repetitions of the facts or your considered opinion will wear even the most aggressive man down eventually.

Don't be side-tracked, don't allow yourself to get angry. Just stick to your point and wear him down with sweet reason.

Learning how to stand your ground

Many women lack assertiveness, perhaps confusing it with aggression. Not only does that cause them difficulties in clashes with work colleagues or superiors, but more generally it can lead to a lack of control over their work environment.

There are a variety of courses now available that are designed to provide individuals with the necessary skills to make the most of themselves, and they are particularly relevant to today's working woman. One small company in the Lake District offers training in assertiveness, decision-making and relationships in the form of an Outward Bound course. The course organisers believe that the practical skills that are acquired during the physical exercises such as canoeing and mountaineering can be carried over to everyday life. Guided group discussions are one of the ways by which the parallels are drawn.

One woman who went on the course believes that she has gained a lot from her three days of strenuous physical activity.

> I can think of a lot of things that I learnt that will help me at work. For instance, that it's all right to feel uncomfortable, scared, nervous and check out a situation and then still go forward and do it. So for new activities in work, that's going to be really useful. Also the ability to say No if I don't want to do something – which I think makes my Yes count for a lot more, because it means I really do want to do it and I am going to do it and put myself into it.
>
> I think that I also learnt to look for a lot more options than I normally do. Instead of just seeing a couple of answers to a problem, I can see a much broader spectrum now and choose them. I also think that it's helped me with people in authority. I feel more comfortable with authority figures now. I feel more equal with them. That came from

the fact that the leaders on this course did most of the activities too.

I'm a very competitive person, that's been my lifestyle up until now, and I think that I've learnt how much more fun and how much more comfortable co-operation is than competition for competition's sake.

Are you a true career woman?

If the following statements were to be made about you, would they be true or false?

My partner's job is more important than mine
It's important that I support him in his career
He has a higher level of formal education than I do
I chose my career with my future family in mind
I would work at a lower level if family demands required
I don't usually describe myself by the job I do

If you've answered a firm 'False' to all of those you can call yourself a career woman, and your relationship with your spouse or partner is one between equals. A 'True' shows you're not at ease with your career plans – perhaps you see them as being too self-serving? But before you abandon all to sacrifice yourself on the altar of marriage, get your partner to answer these questions:

I would be content to be the lesser wage-earner
I'm proud of my partner's skills and achievements
Her ability as a housekeeper isn't important
I would hold back my career if necessary to help advance hers
I do what I can to help her cope both at home and work

Five honest answers of 'True' show you're extremely fortunate in your choice of mate. If you are a 'New Woman', then he's certainly a 'New Man'. One or two 'Falses' – don't worry, he may have feet of clay but at least he's trying!

CHAPTER TEN

How to beat stress at work

What organisations can do

As we have seen, just recognising that they do have a stress problem is a valuable first stage in the recovery of many people suffering from the physical and mental symptoms which often occur during the second extended 'adaptation' stage of the stress response. It is now well established that most people respond well when their symptoms are explained to them in a wider context which helps them to make sense of what's happening to them. They are ready and able to accept informed advice on what steps they can take to alter the circumstances of their working lives, by learning to recognise the sources of their stress and, insofar as they are free to do so, by adopting more sensible and paced styles of working – what's often called 'stress management'. Many of the stress problems of working life are compounded by what's happening to people at home, and they can be given advice and help with these problems too. Finally, they can be encouraged and advised on how to take more exercise, cut down on overeating, smoking and drinking, and adopt basic techniques of relaxation.

All this seems fairly straightforward common sense, but although the connection between the work environment and mental health is now offically accepted by the Health and Safety Executive, since they funded a major study by the Department of Experimental Psychology at Oxford University, there is no great sense of urgency in Britain about developing a health policy on work stress. For example, the House of Lords Select Committee on Science and Technology produced a substantial report on occupational health and hygiene in 1984, but made no mention of work stress, and as yet there is only one scheme in Britain whereby a doctor can refer a patient for such stress therapy under the National Health Service.

The Cambridge Health Authority has announced that it will spend just £4,000 in 1986 to pay for 'trained relaxation leaders' to work in health centres and community health buildings. This follows on from an experiment in 1985 when six Cambridge GPs provided deep breathing relaxation classes which were enthusiastically received.

There are, however, a number of private agencies and associations which offer advice and therapy for individuals suffering from stress, of which the British Holistic Medical Association and the Stress Syndrome Foundation are notable examples. There are also a few private individuals offering exercise and relaxation training, but agencies specifically concerned with stress at work are much less common. For the last two or three years a few management training colleges and firms have run one- or two-day courses on stress management usually aimed at executives of private firms or senior figures in the state-run 'caring' professions like teaching, social work, and nursing.

Recently Dr Malcolm Carruthers of the Positive Health Centre and Dr Christopher Ridgeway of Executive Health Screening, both based in Harley Street, have begun to offer firms basic screening procedures to identify particular employees under stress and provide advice and support for them. The enormously experienced psychology department of the Maudsley Hospital is also assessing the viability of setting up an assessment and advisory service for industry on stress, but all these services operate on a small scale and are of necessity fairly expensive. It costs about £30 each for employees to be tested by the Positive Health Centre, for example. Clearly this kind of approach has a long way to go before it is widely accepted by employers.

One of the most distinguished and successful grass-roots organisations to tackle work stress is The Foundation for the Promotion of Occupational and Mental Welfare which was set up a few years ago by a retired psychiatric social worker, Mrs Peggy Kellam, under the title of 'The Stress at Work Group'. Mrs Kellam set up small local groups in the Midlands around her home in Northampton to provide advice and psychotherapy specifically for people stressed at work, and she has a long record of providing useful help and support for many ordinary workers in a variety of occupations, especially those at her local Plessey factory.

As yet, only a tiny handful of employers in this country offer any formal in-house stress management or advice. Where this does occur it tends to take the form of extending the duties and responsibilities of existing health officers so that they react more positively and swiftly to early warnings of stress among employees. For example, the London City offices of the Trustee Savings Bank have an excellent service of this kind run by their Nursing Welfare Officer, Margaret Watson. Some firms do, however, provide in-house gym facilities – which does at least help towards stress reduction. They include Shell, BP, STC, Sainsbury's, United Biscuits, Rank Xerox (who were pioneers of employee fitness in Britain, opening a gym at their headquarters in 1974) and a number of City banks and finance companies. A very few firms do have an active anti-stress policy or provide the facilities to minimise the effects of stress, but it's no coincidence that they are usually subsidiaries of large American firms like Xerox or Control Data.

Comprehensive stress management programmes are now commonplace throughout American industry, and it has been argued that this has been a major factor in the marked decline of stress-related illness – especially cardiovascular diseases – in the USA over the last ten years. But this extensive and expensive American concern with employees' health doesn't simply reflect an altruistic benevolence on the part of employers. It has been said that the origins of this concern can be dated exactly to a day in 1956 when a machine operator called James Carter, working for General Motors in Detroit, had a nervous breakdown. He explained to his doctors that his breakdown had occurred because he had been unable to keep up with the pace of production-line work, and had been repeatedly criticised by his supervisor, and in 1960 he sued General Motors for compensation for work-related injuries.

The company accepted that his job was indeed stressful but claimed that it was no different in kind from the stresses suffered by all its production-line workers. However, a Michigan Supreme Court jury made the historic decision that the *generality* of the work stress was no argument against Carter's claim that he had suffered from it – and they awarded him compensation. The major step the jury took was to ignore previous rulings that only a 'discrete identifiable accident' could be compensated for, and the concept of 'cumulative trauma' entered the American medical judicial vocabulary.

A few years later a lorry driver called Ted Alcorn won a claim against his employers for the insomnia and nausea he suffered as a result of emotional distress caused by his manager's attitudes (and protests) about his union activities. These and similar cases are now widely used in the USA as the basis for stress-related disability claims, which have now reached vast proportions. In California alone there are more than 3,000 compensation claims every year for work-stress related psychiatric injury, for one in five of all disability claims in this state now relate to 'cumulative trauma'. It has thus become acutely sensible for American firms to provide public and positive evidence of their commitment to employee welfare and stress-control programmes.

Alongside this defensive policy against litigation American employers are made far more aware of the real cost of stress-related employee illness, as they have to provide medical insurance policies and services as well as the ever-increasing costs of replacing highly trained personnel. For example, General Motors had to spend about $2000 a year on each employee – about 1.3 billion dollars in 1978. In simple, pragmatic terms US employers have found it cheaper and more efficient to make every effort to safeguard the health of their employees.

They have used a wide variety of approaches to accomplish this: psychological counselling, on-site keep-fit facilities, relaxation classes, information and training on diet, and extensive medical checks and remedial fitness programmes. It's been estimated by at least one major US firm that the short-term costs of these kinds of facilities can be recouped in terms of reduced absenteeism and sick-leave alone in about ten years.

A number of studies have been made of the effect of these policies on workers, and it's not surprising that they demonstrate a wide variety of benefits not only in the general health and well-being of employees but in their job performance as well – to the gratification of employers.

One of the most ambitious and wide-ranging of the US health programmes has been set up by the massive Control Data Corporation for its 27,000 US employees and their spouses. Control Data – like several other large US firms – now covers its employees' health costs directly itself. Their five-part care programme is called STAYWELL, and is particularly concerned with helping employees to stop smoking, control their weight, improve cardiovascular fitness, manage stress and improve diet. Participation in the scheme is free and voluntary, and so far large numbers of management and blue-collar workers have participated.

What's most striking about the STAYWELL scheme is that it doesn't simply react to ill-health or stress complaints from employees. Each employee begins by accepting a detailed physical screening and giving medical staff a confidential report on his or her lifestyle with particular reference to smoking, drinking and diet. Then each employee has his risk profile explained to him, emphasising what action he might take to reduce his own particular health weaknesses. Finally, the employee decides what courses he wishes to take part in from the variety offered by the company. Control Data claim the results are spectacular and that these policies save them more than $10 million a year net in the USA alone as a result of fewer absences and reduced health-care costs.

In 1980 Control Data decided to offer a modified version of STAYWELL for employees in its subsidiaries in the UK, France and Holland. In 1981, these subsidiaries adopted part of the programme called Employee Advisory Resources – or EAR. The UK division has employees in a wide range of jobs making and distributing business computers. The British EAR is organised and supervised by John Hall.

He explained to us that the service is essentially a counselling and advisory programme which aims to help any and all of the employees and their families with both work and home problems. As in the US system, workers are invited to use a completely confidential 24-hour telephone advice service which, sensibly, is independent of the rest of the company. The EAR mainly provides three kinds of service. Firstly, it provides basic information on all kinds of subjects – especially contacts for more specialised helping agencies outside the company – which may involve quite difficult queries about mortgages or maternity rights or involved personal problems. Secondly, EAR has three in-house trained counsellors to whom employees can talk in person if they wish. These counsellors are supposed to help people to decide if they really have a problem, assess its nature and then outline some options for resolving it. They also act as a short-term support system while people are attempting to resolve their difficulties. John Hall is very keen to emphasise that they don't take on employees' problems. 'At the end of the day, we are here very much to help people to help themselves.' Thirdly, the EAR counsellors will identify and assess people who really do need longer-term help or therapy, and then refer them to appropriate specialised resources in the community.

On top of this, following the American pattern, the EAR service organises seminars and talks intended to anticipate and prevent potential stress problems. These include practical issues like borrowing money and using legal services, as well as common problems ranging from work worries to alcoholism and smoking. The service has been running for four years now, and so far the counselling services have been used by all employees from senior management down. Last year about 500 people called in from all around the country. John Hall is extremely enthusiastic about the benefits of the scheme – both for employees and for Control Data. He claims that the company has already seen a reduction in absenteeism and employee turnover, and an increase in productivity.

We believe that the returns to the company far outweigh the cost of providing the service. It's obviously extremely difficult to quantify the benefits of this programme, but we believe that the benefits are so apparent in human, moral, developmental terms that they don't actually need justifying financially. But we know the benefits are there for individuals who come along with a particular problem. They can save themselves time, money, but more importantly they can save themselves anxiety and stress.

The basic assumption for us being here is that we all have problems. Everybody has problems at some time or another. Those problems affect us not only at home, but they affect us at work. If somebody has a particular problem on their mind, they may be taking time off from work, they may not be working very well. Therefore, if we as a company can provide some help to the people with those problems we're providing a benefit, not only to the individual, but we're also providing a benefit to the company because quite simply, a less troubled employee will work better for Control Data.

As a footnote, Control Data – in true US entrepreneurial fashion – now offers an advisory service to other companies both in this country and America. Thankfully, in the UK a few companies at least are beginning to discuss the EAR scheme with Control Data, and if it is as cost-effective as the Americans claim there seems no reason at all why this should not quickly become a standard element in all British firms' welfare schemes. If it doesn't, it will mean that, unlike the Americans (and indeed employers in every other major Western country), British employers are still wilfully reluctant to appreciate the direct economic and social benefit of such simple schemes to help employees. It would confirm the suspicion of some outside observers that the British simply can't get rid of the idea that being at work must of necessity be a tiring and demanding grind, set against a background of unrelenting dispute between managers and workers.

What *you* can do

Now that you've read through this book you'll have gained a fair idea of what are believed to be some of the main reasons why people become stressed at work, and some of the things that can be done about it. You're in a good position now to carry out what's come to be called a 'stress audit'.

Have a look at the symptoms lists on pages 8 and 12. If you don't seem to be suffering from much stress that's great! But it doesn't mean to say you shouldn't make sure you won't be stressed in future, so keep reading ... and, meantime, take a look around. Do you recognise any stress symptoms in the people who work with you? If you do, you really *should* try to help – and you *can*, by helping that person to carry out some of the stress-treating procedures we've outlined in the book.

So if you, or the people you work with, think from looking at the symptoms lists that one of you is suffering from the effects of stress, what should you do? First of all you should go and see your doctor – immediately – and you should arrange to take a break from work on medical grounds. Some of the stress symptoms might not *look* like the signs of approaching illness, but they all are.

When you come back to work you'll be feeling better, but of course the root of the problem remains untreated. Now you have to decide what to do so that you don't get stressed again. First identify the causes of stress in your workplace. Here are the most common ones.

Decide whether each particular statement describes a source of stress for you at work.

Work overload
Work underload
Time pressures and deadlines
The amount of travel required by my work
Long working hours
Taking my work home
Lack of power and influence
Attending meetings
My beliefs conflicting with those of the organisation
Threat of job loss
Having to move with my job in order to progress my career
Unsympathetic boss
Incompetent boss
Personal relationships with other colleagues
Unrealistic objectives
Demands of work on my relationship with my family
Feeling undervalued
Promotion prospects
Rates of pay
Office politics
Lack of consultation and communication in my organisation

If you are suffering from stress something has to *change* – either your behaviour, or the stressing factors in the place where you work, or both. Perhaps you're in the kind of job where there's not much that can be done to change it for you personally without major changes in the way the whole place is organised. For example, if you have to work on a production line, you may find that that gives you the same kind of personal problems we came across in Chapter Five – but at the same time you can't afford to leave the job. Although the day may be a long time coming when your employers finally see sense and reorganise the way you work into something like the kind of participative, low-stress environments we've discussed, there's still a lot that you and your fellow workers can do to build your own 'stress protection kit'.

Let's look at the things you *can* change that are entirely under *your* control.

Diet. The recognition of stress has helped us to realise that we're not just general-purpose machines with a clever brain on top. People have built-in needs and limits which have to be respected if they are to be happy and healthy. That's because we first evolved to suit a certain kind of lifestyle where we hunted and gathered together in groups in what were probably fairly comfortable conditions. We *can* worry and plan and work terribly hard all the time, but we evolved to use these capacities only *occasionally*. Our earliest ancestors probably strolled around most of the time in what we would consider to be a dangerously relaxed and thoughtless way!

As they drifted about, these amiable groups would spend a lot of time eating – almost anything edible they bumped into. Their stomachs (and ours) evolved to deal with this varied diet. It involved a lot of fibre and vegetables, lots of vitamins, not all that much protein or animal fat – and nothing at all of refined sugar, caffeine or alcohol ... or tranquillisers. So it seems logical that this kind of diet suits us best – particularly if we make sure that we get lots of the foods that contain the B vitamins – the 'anti-stress vitamins' – like wholemeal bread.

Exercise. Exercise is one of the simplest and most direct ways of reducing the effect, of stress, as regular moderate rhythmic exercise has the effect of improving general body fitness and resistance to illness. It strengthens muscles – especially the heart – and, by speeding up the general metabolism and increasing oxygen intake, maintains active growth processes in all our body cells. In relation to stress it functions in a number of useful and specific ways.

Reflecting the way our bodies have evolved so that we are most happy and fit as active busy animals, energetic physical activity carries out the useful function of breaking up and metabolising the fats and sugars released into the bloodstream, especially those produced during periods of stress. At the same time it lowers blood pressure by improving heart function and increasing circulation. Perhaps most important of all, moderate regular exercise decreases cortisol levels in the blood, enhancing the function of the immune system. The noradrenalin produced also makes people feel alert, less tired and aids concentration. Exercise also increases the production of the natural morphine-like substances (endorphins) which give people a pleasant exercise 'high' without recourse to alcohol or smoking. It is also known to relieve depression.

Psychologically, exercise provides an opportunity to escape for a little while from job preoccupations, and can also provide an opportunity to release bottled-up feelings. Meeting their own targets of achievement and improving fitness increase people's self-esteem and, as their general sense of health and well-being (and often their shape) improves, it enhances their positive sense of themselves as attractive and worthwhile people. Probably the most sensible exercises for most people to take part in are moderate running, energetic walking, simple gym exercises and swimming.

Relaxation. A number of techniques of relaxation are now available in this country. They include yoga, meditation of various kinds, autogenics and bio-feedback techniques. What their devotees have in common is the belief that some form of relaxation will reduce the impact of stress. Certainly, many people who try some form of relaxation training report improved feelings of calmness and well being, but does this actually decrease their chances of stress illness? The answer seems to be a very clear Yes. Several studies both in this country and America have demonstrated the beneficial effects of some form of relaxation. As arousal levels are brought down, the sympathetic nervous system ceases to stimulate the production of cholesterol, and the blood pressure tends to go down and stay down.

Some of the most comprehensive studies of this phenomenon have been made by Dr Chandra Patel and her colleagues, including Dr M. G. Marmot and Dr D. J. Terry, working in this country. She became interested in the beneficial effects of meditation when, as a young doctor in the early seventies, she found herself feeling stressed by her own sense of helplessness to cope with the stress-related illness problems of many of her patients. About half of all the people who visit their GP complain of some kind of stress-related illnesses like headaches, stomach problems, breathlessness and raised blood pressure. To help herself she practised the yoga exercises she'd learned as a child, and rapidly found that she felt much better. At that time, in the early seventies, she had one patient with very high blood pressure who had reached a saturation level of anti-hypertensive drugs. She decided to teach this patient some breathing and relaxation exercises and then watched her patient's blood pressure come down quickly and dramatically. 'So much I couldn't believe it.'

She began to try the technique on other hypertensive patients with similarly gratifying results, and in 1973 she began a series of studies of increasing range and scale to confirm this phenomenon. Her most recent study has been of 200 workers known to be at risk of heart disease. They were divided into two groups. Both groups were given routine advice on giving up smoking, losing weight, and eating less animal fat, but one group was also taught simple techniques of basic meditation and relaxation over eight one-hour training sessions. Dr Patel used a simple bio-feedback machine to help them learn to relax. They were also taught some basic stress-management techniques about keeping calm whenever possible and trying to pace the way they worked.

At the end of a four-year period the relaxation group varied in their dedication to the relaxation techniques they'd been taught, but still had, on average, lower blood pressures than the control group that had not been taught relaxation.

Five members of the relaxation group had developed a heart or circulatory disorder in this period, as against nine of the control group – and indeed one of the control group had actually died of a heart attack. The lowered blood pressures of the relaxed group do not account for all the differences in their lower rate of heart illness, and Dr Patel suspects that there are other unrecognised effects of relaxation which are producing this decrease in heart disease. In some curious way the feelings of well-being produced by relaxation seem to be associated with lower rates of disease. An even more recent American study, published this year, confirmed that relaxation training can also increase the activity of the auto-immune system. All this seems to reflect the fact that during relaxation the parasympathetic nervous system is given a chance to balance the arousing activities of the sympathetic nervous system with the various effects that we've previously described in Chapter One.

Relaxation has also been shown to be an aid to simple 'self-hypnosis'. When people are in the still, calm state which is achieved when they have become adept at relaxation, they seem to be able to alter their own basic beliefs and attitudes about themselves more easily than if they try to do this in a normal aroused state. Those who practise autogenics are directed to repeat one positive statement or intention to themselves. This may vary from changing habits ('I am allowed not to drink alcohol every day') to positive attitudes to work ('I will achieve the tasks I set myself at work').

American researchers suggest that even simpler relaxation procedures can have a positive effect. Subjects report an enhanced sense of well-being and a more positive feeling about themselves and their capacities if they just stop for a few minutes regularly each morning and evening, sit quietly with their eyes closed and repeat a word like 'peace' silently to themselves.

Finally, relaxation expert Jane Madders here in the UK reports that many of her clients obtain a calming sense of 'distance' from immediate, less worrying demands, and a gain in their capacity to cope with them, if they simply remember to stop and pause for a few moments. We repeat her instant 'stop emergency technique' here. It's extremely easy to learn and practise, and you never know when you might need it.

When you are getting really worked up:

1 Say 'stop' to yourself.
2 Breathe in deeply and breathe out slowly. As you do so, drop your shoulders and relax your hands.
3 Breathe in deeply again and, as you breathe out, make sure your teeth aren't clenched tightly together.
4 Take two small quiet breaths.

Hobbies. Finally, not having an outside interest is a very good predictor of whether someone is likely to be stressed at work or not.

Enjoy yourself! It is extremely valuable to have other activities and interests outside work – the more different from work the better. Active hobbies like gardening are excellent, but contemplative sports like fishing give you a valuable chance to just sit quietly. As you might expect, we strongly recommend that you don't get too involved in highly competitive activities.

Keeping a pet – especially something that you enjoy stroking – has been shown to be a valuable stress-reducer, particularly for people who live alone. Changes in blood chemistry, of the kind associated with increased activity of the relaxing parasympathetic nervous system, have been detected in people as they spend time with their pets. If you don't live alone, spend as much time as you can with your family – there's lots of evidence that family support is a vital factor in protecting workers from stress.

Let's take a look now at the kinds of action that you personally can take to improve and de-stress your experience when you are actually at work.

The first thing you can do is to sit down and think very carefully whether you are in the right job at all. You may have chosen your career hastily in the first place, or watched the job conditions and demands change around you, or you may have been promoted or moved to a position that simply doesn't suit you. If you regularly feel inadequate or downhearted at work while everyone else around seems to be enjoying it, you may simply be in the wrong job. You *can* change it, and you *should*. One of the clearest conclusions that comes out of all the efforts by psychologists to devise tests and procedures for selecting people for jobs is that if you are doing a job that suits your temperament, you will tend to do it well and relatively effortlessly. People are often extremely reluctant to change their job because, although they might not be happy in it, at least they know where they are. However, as you will have read in Chapter Eight, many people thrown out of work under protest by redundancy or closures discover to their amazement that they can be much happier in a completely different kind of job.

To help you decide, there are occupational consultants who can advise you, but you can do some commonsense research yourself. Think about your favourite hobbies – what is it about them that you most enjoy? Write down a description of the characteristics of the job you do that you most dislike. Turn them around, and you have a job specification list for the job and position you will *most* like. Go to the local library and browse. For example, there are now excellent directories of career opportunities. You could even try the tests in a nice little book called *Know Your Own Mind* by James Green and David Lewis.

However, you may not feel you're in the wrong job – you may not even *feel* stressed, just very busy – but you should still check whether you recognise yourself in the description in Chapter Four of Type As. If you *do* suspect you're a Type A, *don't* be proud of it and don't ignore it. You'll certainly be active, aggressive and healthy if you go on as you are – until the day you suddenly drop dead prematurely.

Of course, you may have looked at our descriptions of Type As and decided you're not one at all – you're just finding the job more than you can cope with. What can you do? First do a stress check on your job situation, using our checklists on pages 29 and 60. These checklists won't tell you anything you didn't suspect already, but at least you've *specified* what your particular problems are, and you will see that there are lots of aspects of your job that *don't* stress you.

Next, get 'stress-aware'. Keep a diary for a few weeks and record all the times when you feel anxious or tired. You'll probably think at first that there's nothing you can do about it, but even if you're in a low-paid, highly supervised job you can complain (and you should) to your supervisor and if necessary your union. Keep complaining until something is done. If you're lucky enough to be in a job where you can do something about your own work-pace, have a look at our recommendations on page 67.

The secret of stress management, as any successful news journalist will tell you, is to *pace* yourself. Set yourself your own clear, personal, realistic objectives, and avoid conflicting goals. Don't work at eleven-tenths of your capacity, if you really have to push – work at nine-tenths. Keep some energy in reserve. Take breaks – never work till you drop. Plan ahead as much as you can, order your priorities and don't be afraid to make lists. If in doubt about what to do decide *now* and act on your decision immediately – you might sometimes be wrong but that's not the end of the world – use the experience and press on, but never look back and reproach yourself. Be flexible, and don't be too hard on yourself if you can only do the job to second-class standards under difficult conditions. That will almost certainly do fine.

You may discover from your 'stress check' that your main problem is how you get on with other people at work, especially your boss. You've got to decide how much of it is your fault. A lot of research has been done on sorting out just which are the important aspects of how people treat each other at work. Psychologist Michael Argyle of Oxford University has drawn up a list of the most important principles for supervisors to follow in developing and maintaining successful relationships with their subordinates:

* Plan and assign work efficiently.
* Keep subordinates informed about decisions affecting them.
* Respect the others' privacy.
* Keep confidences.
* Consult subordinates in matters that affect them.
* Advise and encourage subordinates.
* Fight for subordinates' interests.
* Be considerate about subordinates' personal problems.

He has also drawn up a similar list of principles for subordinates to follow.

* Don't hesitate to question when orders are unclear.
* Use your own initiative where possible.
* Put forward and defend your own ideas.
* Complain first to superiors before going to others.
* Respect others' privacy.
* Be willing and cheerful.
* Don't be too submissive.
* Be willing to accept criticism.
* Keep confidences.
* Be willing to help when requested.

And one for co-workers:

* Accept one's fair share of the work load.
* Respect others' privacy.
* Be co-operative over shared physical working conditions (like light, noise etc.)
* Be willing to help when requested.
* Keep confidences.
* Work co-operatively, despite feelings of dislike.
* Don't denigrate another employee to superiors.

It may be that when you look at these lists you will realise that there are lots of ways you can change your behaviour to improve the atmosphere at work, but what if you realise that other people are getting it wrong and you're a bit worried about standing up to them? There are two major areas in which many people find themselves stressed at work because they lack the social skills to get other people to do what they want. These are the ability to be *assertive* and knowing how to *negotiate*.

Assertiveness

Being assertive is being able to communicate with other people clearly and without misunderstandings. If you have ever come away from a confrontation or conversation feeling that something was left unsaid or unclear, or that either person was tricked, used or made to feel guilty, then one of the participants was not being assertive. If you felt that you had expressed what was important to you and allowed the other person to respond in their own way, then, regardless of the final outcome, you behaved assertively. It is important to remember that being assertive refers to a way of coping with confrontations. It does not mean getting your own way every time or winning some battle of wits against another person. In practice assertive behaviour is usually most likely to produce a result which is generally acceptable to all concerned, without anyone feeling that they have been unfairly treated.

Assertiveness is often wrongly confused with aggression. An aggressive confrontation is when one or both parties attempt to put forward their feelings and beliefs at the expense of others. There may be raised voices, angry personal attacks, emotional blackmail and a complete failure of each to understand the other's point of view. In an assertive confrontation, however, each party stands up for their personal rights, but each shows respect and understanding for the other's point of view. An assertive confrontation is likely to result in fair play on both sides, with each maintaining respect for the other.

The reason why assertiveness may not come naturally is that we often tend to believe that we must talk around a subject or drop hints rather than be direct, or that we must offer excuses or justifications for our actions.

In fact we all have a right to use assertive behaviour in a wide variety of situations. We are often schooled early in life to believe that there are times and places where our own need to express ourselves must take second place. For example, in dealing with specialists, experts, and those in 'privileged positions', we often feel that speaking honestly and assertively is, in some way, 'breaking the rules'. Everybody has certain basic human rights, but we often feel guilty about exercising them. Consider, for example, the following:

1 The right to change your mind and break commitments which have been made.
2 The right to make mistakes.
3 The right to make decisions or statements without having

justifications, or even logical bases.

4 The right not to know about something or not to understand.

5 The right to feel and express emotions, both positive and negative, without feeling that it is weak or undesirable to do so.

6 The right not to get involved with someone else's problems, or even to care about them.

7 The right to refuse demands on you.

8 The right to be the judge of yourself and your own actions and to cope with their consequences.

9 The right to do all of these things without giving any reason at all for your actions.

All of the above are basic human rights which we should feel free to uphold whenever we wish. Just realising this can be a liberating experience in itself. In order to assert these rights effectively we need to be able to listen to the other person, allow them to express themselves and to present clearly our own feelings and opinions. It is important not to make excuses or justifications and to stay on the point of the confrontation.

The following are some basic rules of assertiveness:

Don't

1 Put forward an excuse
2 Apologise profusely for refusing
3 Get sidetracked
4 Be manipulated by emotional blackmail
5 Be tentative with your refusal
6 Be rushed into a decision

Do

1 Accept your right to say no
2 Clarify the issues before deciding
3 Say 'no' firmly and clearly
4 Give reasons not excuses
5 Stand firm in the face of persistence
6 Look for alternative solutions

Like all the other skills, being assertive is something which needs to be practised in a wide variety of settings before it becomes second nature. So, while building up these skills, be on the look-out for situations where you might practise them and do so even though your first attempts may be halting. As you find that using the skills produces more fruitful confrontations, you will improve and develop them until they can be used quite naturally as part of your everyday behaviour at work.

Negotiation

When we think of negotiations, it is usually industrial disputes which spring to mind. But in fact there are many other situations in life when we have to negotiate and make deals. Most of what we do in life ends up being a compromise. We have to fit in with other people around us and make decisions which take into account their needs and preferences. To do this effectively we have to be successful negotiators. This means we need to know how to put forward our opinions, to listen to those of the other person, and to come to an amicable agreement. To this end the following rules apply:

Don't open negotiations while you are angry or irritated.

Don't begin the discussion with an informal or rushed meeting.

Don't just hope that the other person knows what you really want.

Don't make your demands wildly in excess of what you think the other person can manage.

Don't use ultimatums unless you are sure you will follow through your threat.

But do practise the following:

1 Participants should pick a time for negotiation when neither side is rushed or stressed so that both parties are able to concentrate their attentions.

2 It is useful to make a 'presentation of case' so that both parties know exactly what the other wants (or at least what they want the other party to think they want!). This

presentation requires thought and planning so the claim is properly worked out.

3 In planning the initial claim it is worth building in some extra, over and above what you actually want, so that at a later stage you can be seen by the other side to be 'giving ground'. Everyone wants to feel they have got something off the other side so be prepared to 'give' when you are making your initial claim.

4 It is well worth establishing a 'friendly' relationship with the other side particularly if your own case is not too strong. The more friendly you can become as a person the more guilty they will feel about driving a hard bargain.

5 It makes it easier for the other side to 'give in' if you make sure they understand what they are getting out of the deal you propose. Help them to be able to explain to others why they gave in to you. Give them plenty of justification, and a face-saving way out, so they don't feel they have been taken to the cleaners! You are out to get what you want, not to humiliate the other side.

6 A technique sometimes used is for one party to storm out and say, 'either I get what I want or . . .' This technique really is a test of strength, and it's the sort of tactic you can only risk if you know you can last out. It only works as a bluff if you know the other side think they are in a weak position.

7 It is vital that a deal lasts, which means that both parties must be happy with the outcome no matter how hard they have fought to get it. If one side gives in too grudgingly they may go back on the deal later. It helps to re-state the deal at the end of the encounter to ensure that both sides are agreeing the same conditions.

Finally, remember that in a sense all jobs are a kind of *game*. You can play it to win, but whether you win or not the main thing is that, just like in any other game, you should enjoy what you're doing. Try to be kind to yourself. Be flexible. Lots of problems can be resolved simply by taking a fresh look at other ways of solving them, or even deciding that solving them doesn't really matter anyway. It's not the end of the world if the job doesn't get done – but it can be the end of you if you don't reserve your own right to stay within what you know are the limits of your own abilities and energies. In the end, you are your own employer – and only *you* know what are the right terms and conditions for your personal efforts.

Postscript

It's several years now since the idea of stress as a source of illness or death first entered the consciousness of the average working man or woman, and yet in many ways our thinking about it has hardly moved on at all. Stress is still regarded by many people as a rather intangible if not downright disreputable phenomenon, a handy catch-all for all the moans, resentments and frustrations of people who can't or won't cope with the tough demands of the real world of work and effort. Yet, as we have shown in this book, stress illness is now recognised by scientists and doctors as a real, pervasive and disruptive force in almost every aspect of life – and particularly in the area of work.

We believe that this disparity in acceptance reflects the fact that our thinking about people and the meaning of the work they do is in a period of transition. Until relatively recently we were used to thinking of work as a form of struggle – a necessary evil by which human beings wrested a precarious living from the unforgiving earth, and sometimes in the process exploited and abused one another. However, while recognising the many injustices and cruelties of the world of work, many people were still able to see themselves as dignified by their own particular participation in this dreadful game – developing skills, even if they were only the skills of survival. People at work establish traditions, values and priorities – maintaining careers which gave shape and direction to their lives.

Increasingly, however, many of us have to consider skilled and meaningful work as a *privilege*, and any work at all as a considerable benefit. Among manual workers, miners nowadays have to go on strike to fight for the right to work in difficult and dangerous conditions in pits which are theoretically not worth keeping open. Many other groups of workers, including shipbuilders and steelworkers, have already lost that fight. Unskilled women now frequently replace skilled men in order to carry out assembly jobs which are deliberately made as much like a machine process as possible so that the mistakes they make will resemble machine errors – constantly repeated, easily spotted and quickly remedied. These production-line assembly jobs are on the increase rather than the decrease because we now understand that they represent the transitional period between skilled construction methods and completely roboticised production.

At managerial levels the pace and range of demands has increased, and the rate of change has also increased. But these new strains are often added to jobs which themselves originally evolved in a haphazard and insightless way. Our commitment to economic expansion – coupled with increasing productivity based on technological developments – means that it's not only assembly workers whose lives are paced by machines. In a real sense we *all* are – and increasing numbers of us simply can't cope.

The new recognition of the phenomenon of stress may well prove to be as valuable as the realisation of the connection between epidemic disease in British cities of the early nineteenth century and the state of their water supplies and sewage systems. We are reluctant to accept the reality of stress not only because (unlike noise or pollution) it's difficult to identify, but also because it demonstrates our vulnerability and reminds us that the fact that we all agree that a job is humanly possible doesn't necessarily mean that it will not ultimately be damaging to humans.

If we did not have the destructive effects of stress to observe we might well carry on demanding the impossible in various ways of many of the people who cheerfully commit themselves to work far more than the nine to five in order to earn their daily bread.

It may well be that through the very fact of stress, and the damage that we have to recognise that it causes, we can all look forward to a time when the first priority in organising the way we work will have to be what it should always have been – ensuring that each and every one of us is engaged in worthwhile and purposeful effort which doesn't just bring in a wage but gives enjoyment, value and meaning to our lives.

Useful organisations

Baynards House
1 Chepstow Place
City of Westminster
London W2 4TF
Tel: 01 229 3456
*Promotes and encourages health
and safety at work.*

**The British Association for
Counselling**
37A Sheep Street
Rugby
*Referral service to local
counsellors.*

**British Association of
Occupational Therapists**
20 Rede Place
City of Westminster
London W2 4TU
Tel: 01 299 9738
Advice and information.

**Employment Medical Advisory
Service**
1 Long Lane
Southwark
London SE1 4PG
Tel: 01 407 8911
*Service of doctors and nurses who
will advise on fitness for training
or employment.*

Executive Health Screening
148 Harley Street
London W1
*Stress screening using computer
based questionnaire plus medical
examination. Stress counselling
and referral.*

Family Link Line/Network
60 Maiden Lane
Clubmoor
Liverpool
Merseyside L13
Tel: 051 256 7042
*Confidential listening service for
families and individuals under
stress.*

Families Under Stress
0653 86256 – telephone only.
*Support and information for
families under stress.*

Foundation for Living
494 Kenton Road
Kenton
Harrow
Middlesex
HA3 9DL
Tel: 01 204 6524
*Relaxation courses, stress control
techniques and meditation*

Industrial Health Service
Nuffield House
College Road
Rochdale
Greater Manchester OL12 6AE
Tel: 0706 48855
Help support and advice.

The Industrial Society
Peter Runge House
3 Carlton House Terrace
London SW1Y 5DG
Tel: 01 839 4300

Industrial Therapy Organisation Ltd
Lydstep Terrace
Dean Lane
Bristol
Avon BS1 1DR
Tel: 0272 668491
Help for those with occupational illness.

International Stress and Tension Control (I.S.T.C.A.)
14 Cranleigh Avenue
Rottingdean
Brighton
Sussex BN2 7GT
Help advice and information.

Jane Madders' Relaxation Tape
Available for £5 from:
Relaxation for Living
29 Burwood Park Road
Walton-on-Thames
Surrey KT12 5LH
Tel: 09322 27826
Also provides courses, including correspondence courses. Teachers throughout UK.

Lifeskills
3 Brighton Road
Barnet
London N2
Tel: 01 346 9646
Self-help cassettes developed by behavioural psychologists to control tension, etc.

Lifeskills Associates
Ashling
Back Church Lane
Leeds
LS16 8DN
Publications and workshops on career and life management.

Lifestyle Training Centre Ltd
23 Abingdon Road
Kensington and Chelsea
London W8
Tel: 01 938 1011
Offers a range of cassettes on anxiety and stress management (£6.00 cost).

Maisner Centre
41 Preston Street
Brighton
East Surrey BN1 2AP
Tel: 0273 729818
The centre runs courses in progressive relaxation therapy. These courses do cost.

Mind
National Association for Mental Health
22 Harley Street
London W1N 2EP
Tel: 01 637 0741

Open Door
Social Centre
Gosforth Lane
South Oxhey
Hertfordshire
Tel: 01 428 2483
*Open to all who are lonely and
suffering from stress and tension.*

Positive Health Centre, The
101 Harley Street
City of Westminster
London W1
Tel: 01 935 1811
*Autogenic training courses for
stress management.*

Relaxation Close
10 Pond Close
Norwich
Norfolk
Tel: 0607 811 077
Help, advice and information.

Relaxation for Living
29 Burwood Park Road
Walton-on-Thames
Surrey KT12 5LM
Tel: 0932 227826
*Runs relaxation classes either for
personal caller or by
correspondence.*

Skills with people
15 Liberia Road
London N5 1JD
Tel: 01 359 2370
*Training: specialising in running
courses about communication.*

Society of Occupational Medicine
Royal College of Physicians
11 St Andrew's Place
Camden
London NW1
Tel: 01 486 2641
Help, advice and information.

**Society for the Prevention of
Asbestosis and Industrial Diseases**
38 Drapes Road
Enfield
Middlesex EN2 8LU
Tel: 0707 873025
*Works on preventing asbestosis and
other industrial diseases.*

**Society of Teachers of the
Alexander Technique**
3 Albert Court
Kensington Gore
Kensington and Chelsea
London SW7
Tel: 01 589 3834
*A professional organisation
teaching stress control.*

Stress Syndrome Foundation, The
Cedar House
Yalding
Kent ME18 6JD
Tel: 0622 814431
Help, advice and information.

Stress Watch
PO Box 4 AR
City of Westminster
London W1A 4AB
Help, advice and information.

Stress at Work
9 Abington Park Crescent
Northampton
NN3 3AD
Tel: 0604 326675
*Confidential advice and support by
professionals to both organisations
and individuals.*

Trancendental Meditation
Roydon Hall
East Peckham
Nr. Tonbridge
Kent TN12 5HN
Tel: 0622 812121
*Please send s.a.e. for introductory
leaflet and details of courses in
your area.*

Work Hazards Group
British Society of Social
Responsibility in Science
(BSSRS)
9 Poland Street
City of Westminster
London W1V 3DG
*Involved in occupational health
issues.*

Work Research Unit
St Vincent House
30 Orange Street
London WC2H 7HH
Tel: 01 839 9281

Yoga
The Yoga for Health Foundation
Ickwell Bury
Nr. Biggleswade
Bedfordshire
Tel: 076 727 271
*For information on local clubs and
centres throughout the country.*

Select Bibliography

Argyle, Michael, *The Social Psychology of Work* (Penguin, 1981)
— *Social Skills and Work* (Methuen, 1981)
Cooper, Cary L., *The Stress Check* (Prentice-Hall, 1981)
—and Marshall, J., *Understanding Executive Stress* (Macmillan, 1978)
—and Payne, R., *Stress at Work* (John Wiley, 1978)
Coleman, Vernon, *Stress Control* (Pan, 1978)
Green, James and Lewis, David, *Know Your Own Mind* (Pelican, 1983)
Hodgson, Ray and Miller, Peter, *Self-Watching: Addiction, Habits, Compulsions, What to do about them* (Century Publishing, 1982)
Macdonald, Janet, *Climbing the Ladder: How to be a Woman Manager* (Methuen 1986)
Madders, Jane, *Stress and Relaxation* (Martin Dunitz, 1981)
Littler, Craig R., *The Experience of Work* (Gower for Open University, 1985)
Nicholson, John and Lucas, Martin, *All in the Mind* (Thames Methuen, 1984)
Poteliakhoff, Alex and Carruthers, Malcolm, *Real Health* (Davis-Poynter, 1981)
Spielberger, C., *Understanding Stress and Anxiety* (Harper and Row, 1979)
Sharpe, Dr R. and Lewis, David, *Thrive on Stress* (Souvenir Press, 1977)
Thompson, Dr Richard, *Pocket Guide to Stress* (Arlington Pocket Books)
Tryer, Dr Peter, *Stress* (Sheldon Press, 1980)
Wood, Clive, *Living in Overdrive* (Fontana, 1984)
Duck, Dr Steve, *Friends for Life* (Harvester Press, 1985)
Back, Ken and Kate, *Assertiveness at Work* (McGraw-Hill)
Kniveton, Dr Bromley and Towers, Dr B., *Training for Negotiating* (Basic Books)
Lineham, Dr Marsha and Egan, Dr Kelly, *Asserting Yourself* (Century Publishing, 1983)
Consumers' Association, *Living with Stress* (CA, 1982)

Index

references in **bold type** are to checklists, tables or questionnaires

absenteeism as index of stress, 13, 26
addiction, 15
  'stress addiction', 9–10
adrenalin, 9, 17, 23, 24
aggression, 159 *see also* Type A
  personalities
ambition, 53 *see also* Type A
  personalities
anxiety, 5–6, 23, 31
apathy, 14
APEX, 25
appraisal of stress, 23–24
arousal, 23, 31, **60**
assembly-line work *see* blue-collar
  workers
assertiveness, 158–161, **159–160**
  assertiveness training, 141–142
ASTMS, 25
attitude, 70, 83–84
auto-immune system, 18–21

behaviour modification, 46–48, 64–65
  see also stress, prevention and
  cure
behavioural symptoms of stress, 12–16
  addiction, 15
  apathy, 14
  denial, 15
  displacement, 13
  fantasy, 14
  specialisation, 14
behaviourism, 38–41
biofeedback, 152
blue-collar workers, problems of, 79–
  86, 99

boredom, 6
British Holistic Medical Association,
  144
bureaucracies, 103, 109–110 *see also*
  organisations

cancer, stress as cause of, 17, 21
career development, 127
career plateaus, 127
careers
  career break scheme, 133–135
  dual career family, 137–139,
    139
  mid career crisis, 127
caring, stress of professional change,
  101ff, 113ff
  ability to cope with, **118–119**
  adapting to, 113–114
  coping skills, 127–128, **128**
  deskilling, 122–127
  guidelines for introducing, **126**
  Life Change stresses, 116–119
  mechanism of adaptation to, 113–
    114
clients, working for, 95–97
communication, importance of, 109–
  112 *passim*
competitiveness, 57
computers, 123, 125
  women and, 135–136
control, 24, 72ff, 121–122
Control Data Ltd, 145, 147–149
  'EAR', 147–148
  Staywell scheme, 147–148
cortisol, 23, 24

counselling, 46–51, 53 *see also* specific
    problems
cumulative trauma, 145–146

danger, perception of, 10–11
'decision latitude', 72 *see also* control
denial, 15 *see also* behavioural
    symptoms
depersonalisation, 93–95
depression, 11, 48–49 *see also* mental
    symptoms
    in adaptation to change, 113–115
    and illness, 21
diet, 151
displacement, 13
dual career families, 137–139, **139**, **142**

emotional burnout, 101ff
    causes, 102
    prevention, 108, **112**
'emotional labourers', 101–102
employers *see* organisations
employee care, 26 *see also* stress,
    prevention and cure
endorphins, 152
executive health screening, 43, 144
exercise, 151–152

fantasy, 14
F International, 135–136
Ford, Dagenham, 81–82

gestalt therapy, 98
group therapy, 98–99

heart attacks *see* heart disease
heart disease
    among blue collar workers, 82
    in Japanese ethnic groups, 88
    mechanism of, 63–64
    prevention of, 64–68 *see also* stress,
        prevention and cure
    and social support, 88, 90, 95–96
    stress implicated in, 17–18, **19**, **20**
    among white-collar workers, 33–35
        see also Type A personalities
    in women, 139–140

Hippocrates, 37
hobbies, 155
homeostasis, 7
home workers, 135–136
housework, 136–137

illness, stress and, 6–7, 16–22, 31–33
    among blue-collar workers, 33, 82
    cancer, 17, 21
    caused by change, 116–119
    economic effects, 21–22
    friendlessness, 88
    heart attacks, 16, 17–18, **19–20**, 33
        see also heart disease
    immune system, 18–21
    and Type A behaviour, 58–64
    in white-collar workers, 33–35
    in women, 136
Inland Revenue, effects of cuts on, 73–
    75
in-house stress management, 145–149
interpersonal skills training, 98

job fit, 41ff
    and personality, 42–45
job satisfaction, 27ff, **29**
    and anxiety, 31
    and arousal, 31
    and bureaucracy, 103
    and control, 83–85
    Which? survey, **28**, 27–29
    job stress 'league table', **30**
job security, 120

life change stresses, 116–119, 117–119
load, 9–10, 47, 73ff
loneliness at work, 96–97 *see also*
    relationships

maternity leave, limitations of, 134
management *see under* careers, illness,
    relationships, organisations
management style, 93–95, 97
managers, problems of, 56–60 *see also*
    relationships
manual workers *see* blue-collar
    workers

Maudsley Hospital, 144
meditation, 152, 153–154
mental symptoms of stress, 10–12, **12**, 101
mid career crisis, 127
minds, effect of stress on *see* mental symptoms of stress

National Health Service, 143–144
National Westminster Bank, 133–135
negotiation, 161–163, **161–162**
neuroticism, 68–69
new technology, 123–127, 135–136
    acceptance by workers, 126
    guidelines for introducing, 126
    job satisfaction, 125
noradrenalin, 9–10, 17, 23, 24, 63–64, 152

occupations
    VDU operator, 11–12, 93–95
    air hostess, 91, 93
    air traffic controller, 89–90
    banking, 132–135
    bus driver, 95–96
    death rates (of various occupations), 32
    dentist, 96–97
    electronics, 14
    farmer, 114–116
    financial consultant, 129, 140
    foremen (supervisors), 77–79, **79**
    hospital porter, 10, 107–108
    journalist, 9–10, 15
    manager, 16, 59–60, 65–67
    new technology, 123, 125
    nurse, 102, 109ff
    office worker, 41, 72–77, **75**, **76**, 90
    pilot, 91–92, 97
    production line, 14, 80–86, **85**
    road mender, 121
    salesman, 57–58
    secretary, 11, 93–94
    shop floor worker, 79–80
    social worker, 14, 105–107
    steel worker, 120
    tax officer, 74–75, 90
    teacher, 103–105, 108–109
    theatre director, 48
    trade union official, 47–48
    waiter, 101
office politics, 89
office work, problems of, 72–77, **75**, **76**
organisations
    conflict of aims, **103**, 103, 108
    role in beating stress, 143–149
    supportive, **99–100**, **112**, 145–149
outward bound courses, 141–142

pace of work, 76–77
parasympathetic nervous system, 9
parents, influence of, 48–49
part time work, 129, 135–137
participation, 83
Pavlov, 37
perfectionism, 47–48
personality problems, 52–53
personality types, 52–53, **54–56**
    ambitious ('Type A'), 53 *see also* Type A personalities
    cancer and, 17
    'hardy', 70
    extrovert, 39
    introvert, 39, 69
    obsessional, 52
    stimulus seeking, 39, 53
    stress prone, 44, 68–70
    unassertive, 52
personality, effect of early experience on, 45–50, 69–70
personnel selection, 42–44
pets, 155
physical stressors, 33
physical symptoms of stress, **8**, 8–10, 94, 95 *see also* illness
physiology
    effects of stress, 23, 24
    and response to stress, 40, 45
Positive Health Centre, 22, 144
positive stress, 22–24, 119–121
Powys Health Authority, 109–112
pressure *see* load
production-line work, 14, 80–86, **85**

[174] Index

psychogenic illness, 15
public spending cuts, effects of, 73–74

redundancy and illness, 7, 116 *see also*
    unemployment
relationships
    lack of, 96
    not a cure-all, 99
    organisational support, 98, **99**, **100**
    with clients, 95–96
    with colleagues, 89–91, **100**
    with managers, 74–75
    poor, effects of, 87ff
    with subordinates, 91–93
    with superiors, 93–95
relaxation, 152–155
    'Stop Emergency technique', 154–
    155, **155**
    meditation, 152, 153–154
responsibility, 6
role conflict, 78, 132–133

security, 120
self-esteem, 107–109
smoking, 15–16
'social readjustment scale', 116–118,
    117
social support
    and health, 87–88
    informal networks, 96, **100**, 105–106
        see also relationships
    organisational *see* organisations,
        relationships
status, 107–109, 110ff, 137
stereotypes, male–female, 131–133
    dangers of, 139–141
'stress audit', 149ff
Stress Syndrome Foundation, 144
stress management, 143, 155–158, **157**,
    158
stress prone personalities, 68–70
stress therapy groups, 144
stress *see also* physical symptoms of
    stress, mental symptoms of stress,
    stress management
    adapting to, 7
    addiction to, 9–10

cumulative trauma, 146
detection, 22
effect on body, 8–9
effect on mind, 10–11
identifying sources at work,
    150
prevention and cure
    organisation's role, 143–149
    self-help, 149–163 *see particularly*
        relaxation, exercise, diet
structured interviews, 62
supervisors, 77–79
sympathetic nervous system, 7

team work, value of, 89–91, 105–107,
    111
therapy, **51**
trade unions, 25–26, 123
Transactional Analysis, 98
Trebor Ltd, 83–85
Type A personalities, 53, 56–68
    'Type A environment', **60**
    identifying, 61, **62**
    illness, 63
    remedies, 64–68, **67–68**
    women, 140
Type B personalities, 58, 63 *see also*
    Type A personalities

unemployment, 7, 26–27, 88, 121–122

VDUs, stress of operating, 93–95 *see*
    also occupations
violence, 13
Volvo, 85

'Woman's work', 136–137
women
    assertiveness, 141
    career breaks, 133–135
    career woman checklist, **142**
    heart attacks, **20**, 139–140
    and new technology, 123, 135–
        136
    percentage at work, 129
    role conflict, 132–133
    smoking, 15–16

stereotyped attitudes to, 131–132
working mothers, 132–135, 137–139
work, functions of, 119–22

wrong job *see* job fit

yoga, 152

Forthcoming titles in Methuen Paperbacks

BARRIE SHERMAN

Working at Leisure

This follows on from the two challenging and thought-provoking books that Barrie Sherman wrote with Clive Jenkins. When *The Collapse of Work* was published in 1979 it found an instant response, and many of its prophecies have already come true. *The Leisure Shock* followed two years later and tried to prepare people for the increased leisure time that would inevitably result from unemployment and the new work patterns.

Barrie Sherman assesses in *Working at Leisure* the developments that have taken place since then, both in the workplace and at home (the new leisure centre). He emphasises that our only hope for the future is to realise that we are witnessing the start of a second industrial revolution that will have consequences every bit as far-reaching as the first. We must put aside our outdated preconceptions and recognise that the action we take now could lead us in one of two directions – to widespread unemployment and misery, or to a Brave New World where, for the first time in history, men and women will be able to find fulfilment by balancing their lives equally between work and leisure.

In this brilliant and perceptive analysis Barrie Sherman stresses that we must allow ourselves the luxury of optimism when confronting the future. It is people who will determine what happens to us all – not technology.

Forthcoming titles in Methuen Paperbacks

JANET W. MACDONALD

Climbing the Ladder

How to be a Woman Manager

'Nice girls don't compete, they sit politely and wait to be chosen. Generations of women have grown up convinced that if they do their best, they will be noticed and rewarded, then wondered why the rewards were not forthcoming.'

Since the early 1970s the number of women gaining high-level posts and high-level salaries has been steadily increasing, but progress is still very slow. There is no logical or physiological reason why a woman should not run a major international company, but there are a number of psychological reasons why few succeed in doing so.

Three main enemies must be fought if women want their share of opportunity: the company – its history, structure and attitudes; men – both in the office and in private life; and themselves – their self-respect, self-image, self-confidence, their vision of what they want from life and their desire and determination to attain it. And many women are their own worst enemies.

This book will enable all women to recognise and defeat these enemies by drawing up a battle-plan to give the basics of career planning, time management, home life management and the management of relationships with superiors, peers and staff.

It may be harder for women to climb the corporate ladder than for men, but once they have put into practice the sound advice in this book, they will find that the view from the top far outweighs the effort of climbing.